Remaining Faithful

Remaining Faithful

Meditations
on Being True to Yourself
Your Relationships
and Your Principles
from the Bahá'í Sacred Writings

Compiled
with Reflections by
Phyllis K. Peterson

Remaining Faithful

Meditations on Being True to Yourself
Your Relationships
and Your Principles
from the Bahá'í Sacred Writings

Compiled with reflections by
Phyllis K. Peterson

© 2012 Phyllis K. Peterson

All quotations from the Bahá'í Writings used by permission.

ISBN# 978-1888547-50-4

Published by Special Ideas
PO Box 9
Heltonville IN 47436

www.bahairesources.com

Table of Contents

Foreword

Introduction   1

How to Use This Book   8

Meditations:

1	Why we need the Teachings of the Prophets of God	11
2	Me? A Saint who could subdue the cities of men's hearts?	19
3	Support for the Natural Human Condition	23
4	What Maintains the Order of the World?	27
5	Through the Holy Spirit We shall become the Light of the World	31
6	Bahá'u'lláh has Claimed the Hearts of Mankind as His Own	35
7	The Importance of Fidelity	41
8	Don't be Shaken by the Tumult of Tests	45
9	What do I give up to Cleave unto Righteousness?	49
10	Freedom, Responsibility and Chastity	53
11	Connecting My Heart to Bahá'u'lláh	57
12	Verily Thy Lovers Thirst for Chastity!	61
13	Detachment from Divergent Views of Sexual Behavior in the World	65

14	Of Saints and Trusted Servants	71
15	A Saint in a State of Grievous Abasement?	75
16	Let Each Morn Be Better than Its Eve	79
17	If I Add up My Accomplishments Each Day, I Will Feel the Confirmations of God Supporting Me	83
18	Strong Language from a Father Figure	89
19	Am I a Bahá'í in Name Only?	95
20	May all the Latent Fragrant Flowers in My Heart Become Reality	99
21	The Goals are Insight and Detachment, Vision and Upliftment!	103
22	The Raiment of the Human Heart is the Fear of God	107
23	Fulfilling God's Purpose on Earth	111
24	How Much Am I Prepared to Sacrifice? How Sincere Am I?	115
25	Tarry Not!	119
Last Thoughts		125
Appendix		127
References		129
Acknowledgments		136

Foreword:

We live in a world full of temptation, fantasy and hedonism. It is difficult, sometimes, to remain focused on what is real, lasting and of value when the rest of the world sings its siren song of self-gratification and easy familiarity. This is a book created to help people who are struggling to remain faithful to their primary relationship.

Knowing what is right is one thing. Being able to *do* what is right in the face of temptation and disappointments is another. *Doing* what is right requires the kind of soul-level understanding that comes from combining the *inspiration* of the Creative Word with the *insight* born of reflection.

For inspiration, this book looks to the Writings of Bahá'u'lláh, Prophet-Founder of the Bahá'í Faith, and the explanations provided by His son, 'Abdu'l-Bahá. The Bahá'í Faith is the most recent of the world's major religions, starting in 1863, and is already one of the most wide-spread. It teaches that there is only one God, Who loves all of humanity equally, and that all of the major religions were brought by Messengers of this same God.

Bahá'u'lláh wrote hundreds of books and letters covering a myriad different topics. In order to get the most out of *this* book, however, you would benefit from knowing just a few basics about Bahá'u'lláh's teachings on the human condition.

First and foremost, Bahá'u'lláh taught that humans are essentially good and noble, but are in need of guidance and are prone to waywardness. We are spiritual beings who are easily distracted by physical reality and need to be constantly reminded of our higher nature. Fortunately, He taught that God is both just and merciful.

Bahá'u'lláh explained that there is an afterlife, but that Heaven and Hell are metaphors for nearness to God and distance from God.

In Bahá'í ethics, love, justice, compassion, unity, service and the Golden Rule are primary spiritual laws, but purity, chastity, faithfulness and nobility are still required virtues as well. In other words, being nice does not exempt us from the need for sexual morality. Failure to acquire moral virtues in this life will have an effect on our souls when we reach the afterlife.

We are responsible for using our own Free Will to follow God's guidance and strive to become the best people possible in all areas of our lives.

The Writings of Bahá'u'lláh inspire us to try to acquire these virtues, but success depends upon our internalizing them through reflection. To that end, Phyllis Peterson has interspersed these quotations with thought-provoking reflections, questions, observations and personal experiences. It is our hope that reading the quotations and then contemplating the accompanying meditations will help you inscribe the wisdom of Bahá'u'lláh's teachings on your very soul.

— Justice St. Rain

Introduction

"O people of the world. Follow not the promptings of the self for it summoneth insistently to wickedness and lust. Follow rather Him who is the Possessor of all created things, Who biddeth you to show forth piety and manifest the fear of God. He, verily, is independent of all His creatures. Take heed that ye do not stir up mischief in the land after it hath been set in order. Whoso acteth in this way is not of us and we are quit of him"
— Bahá'u'lláh [1]

"O Divine Providence! Bestow Thou in all things purity and cleanliness upon the people of Bahá. Grant that they be freed from all defilement, and released from all addictions. Save them from committing any repugnant act, unbind them from the chains of every evil habit, that they may live pure and free, wholesome and cleanly, worthy to serve at Thy Sacred Threshold and fit to be related to their Lord."' — Abdu'l-Bahá [2]

It was during the Fast that I first read the above passages. And they stopped me in my tracks. "Who so acteth in this way is not of us, and we are quit of him." This sounds like a wrathful God. We don't want to think of God's anger, especially those of us who have been spiritually abused.[3] Yet Bahá'u'lláh is telling us plainly in the Book of Laws that if we go beyond our limits after He has set our lives in order, there will be a severe penalty, a loss.

We have to consider also that He has placed this quote directly between several passages on marriage. God had set my life in order and given me a wonderful husband, so at the moment I opened the Kitab-i-Aqdas to this passage, I felt shame because I realized I was consumed with/distracted by idle fancies and vain imaginings about a man other than my husband. It had started innocently enough...gentle teasing, special smiles and soon I was looking forward to seeing him every day....and then having romantic feelings which led to romantic fantasies, and then to physical sexual feelings.[4] This quotation made me realize I was repeating an old pattern. A veil had been removed by the Aqdas and all my fantasies shimmered into dust. I was left with the shame.

These are things Bahá'ís don't want to talk about. Who do you share it with? How do you stop desire and passion once it has started? I didn't act it out, but I certainly had "idle fancies and vain imaginings" about it. I couldn't help but wonder — who else has these distressful, repetitive thoughts and ongoing fantasies? Was it just me?

All my Bahá'í life, I have turned to the Writings to pray and meditate. *"I adjure thee by thy might O my God! Let no harm beset me in times of tests and in moments of heedlessness* guide my steps aright through thine inspiration,"*[5] Because of my alarm at my heedlessness, I memorized the quotation from the Kitab-i-Aqdas, and then I started compiling quotations for a work that would be both reflective and meditative. Much guidance for the way we live our lives may seem brilliant, but it needs to be tested by holding it up to a higher standard, a higher authority. I consider Bahá'u'lláh to be the Highest Authority, the newest Messenger from God.

*unawareness

"These are the ordinances of God that have been set down in the Books and Tablets by His Most Exalted Pen. Hold ye fast unto His statutes and commandments, and be not of those who, following their idle fancies and vain imaginings, have clung to the standards fixed by their own selves, and cast behind their backs the standards laid down by God." Bahá'u'lláh [6]

I shared this dilemma with a Bahá'í friend, Mahin Pouryaghma, a therapist, who encouraged me to go one step further and share it with my husband. I was fearful of the consequences of revealing this experience, but I also felt confident that somehow he would understand and still trust me. Trust has always been the glue that has held our marriage together. So I told him. He listened quietly and attentively. Then I asked him if he had ever had an experience like mine. He responded with something that made me feel very grateful and very human. He said simply, "I won't tell you any names if you don't tell me any names!" My guilt and shame diminished; and my desire to be faithful increased. So did my desire to be obedient to the commandments of Bahá'u'lláh, and trust in the "fear of God."

This level of honesty must come with a warning, however! Not all spouses will be as accepting as mine – especially if the attraction has been acted upon. Then it becomes an even greater test. What if my husband had recoiled, been accusatory, or confessed with names, or laughed, or threatened me in some way? These all happen in the real world... even with Bahá'ís.[7]

I tried to think what could have made me think my temptation would be "ok", why I didn't anticipate consequences. Such self-honesty is part of bringing oneself to account each day. It is clear to me with hindsight that I had failed to do so.

Faithful

"Bring thyself to account ere thou art summoned to a reckoning, on the Day when no man shall have strength to stand for fear of God, the Day when the hearts of the heedless ones shall be made to tremble." — Bahá'u'lláh[8]

This quotation is a protection for us now and in the future.

I also decided to cling to the Báb's prayer for protection with all my might:

"Immeasurably exalted art Thou, O Lord! Protect us from what lieth in front of us and behind us, above our heads, on our right, on our left, below our feet and every other side to which we are exposed. Verily, Thy protection over all things is unfailing." — The Báb [9]

About two years ago I received a telephone call from a woman who had worked diligently to bring the cluster in which she lived to "A" status. She told me that her husband was having an affair with a seeker; and she was frantic. She didn't know where to turn to save her marriage. She sought me out because of my book "Assisting the Traumatized Soul." She even told me that she would purchase an airline ticket to bring me to counsel her and her husband. Unfortunately, I had no answers for her at that time, aside from telling her to consult with her Local Spiritual Assembly. There simply weren't any good materials available within the Bahá'í Community to help people deal with this difficult issue.

I am sharing my experience here so that she and others might have some hope to cling to.

This book has been compiled not as a self help book, but more purely to stimulate individual reflection, which can take the reader to whatever further specific applications of the Writings and any further actions that may come to them in the course of private meditation. It is a reflective guide for those who are suffering from sexual temptation, shame for feelings of attraction or acting-out, or anger over a partner's infidelity. It includes passages regarding the nobility of man and his high station should he choose to act with righteousness for the sake of God. And it includes the most direct definition of what chastity encompasses, from the pen of Shoghi Effendi, 'Abdu'l-Bahá's grandson.

"Such a chaste and holy life, with its implications of modesty, purity, temperance, decency, and clean-mindedness, involves no less than the exercise of moderation in all that pertains to dress, language, amusements, and all artistic and literary avocations. It demands daily vigilance in the control of one's carnal desires and corrupt inclinations. It calls for the abandonment of a frivolous conduct, with its excessive attachment to trivial and often misdirected pleasures. It requires total abstinence from all alcoholic drinks, from opium, and from similar habit-forming drugs. It condemns the prostitution of art and of literature, the practices of nudism and of companionate marriage, infidelity in marital relationships, and all manner of promiscuity, of easy familiarity, and of sexual vices. It can tolerate no compromise with the theories, the standards, the habits, and the excesses of a decadent age. Nay rather it seeks to demonstrate, through the dynamic force of its example, the pernicious character of such theories, the falsity of such standards, the hollowness of such claims, the perversity of such habits, and the sacrilegious character of such excesses."
— *Shoghi Effendi* [10]

The realization that we have failed to live up to this standard could cause many of us to spiral into hopelessness, wondering if we are, indeed, *true* Bahá'ís. So I also want to address "self-punishment and guilt." Bahá'u'lláh, the Blessed Beauty, consented to be in chains so that we could be free. He came for the happiness of the whole world. He wants us to be happy. The Master, 'Abdu'l-Bahá, also wants us to be happy. Remember? He always asked Bahá'ís if they were happy. So it is our duty to be happy as a thanks giving and duty to him. This means that we must not allow ourselves to be stuck in the prison of self. This door opens from inside and we have the key. We must stop self-punishment and believe we are noble. As the Bible says, God forgives all our sins. If we fail to forgive *ourselves*, it will be considered disobedient. After all, who are *we* to hold a grudge against ourselves while *He* forgives us? Not forgiving ourselves is a sign of arrogance toward Him on our part. We must be humble even about our failings. Our sin is not greater than God's capacity to forgive and show us grace! This is illustrated in the Qu'ran in this quotation:

"Faithful believers, be wary of God and believe God's Messenger: God will give you a double portion of mercy divine, and provide you a light by which to walk; and God will forgive you. And God is the epitome of forgiveness and mercy: That the people of the Book may know they have no power over anything of God's grace; and that the grace is in the hand of God, who gives it to anyone at will. And God has the Great Grace."[11]

Accepting God's forgiveness, of course, does not change the need for His laws. Bahá'u'lláh brought us a Book of Laws to help us to create Unity in the World. So breaking His Laws is a way we contribute to disunity - in our integrity, our relationships, our family, our community. We are rendered less able to be pure examples among the people of the world. Happiness — true happiness — requires us to be free from these conflicts. If we *really* want to avoid getting stuck in guilt, we need to commit ourselves to stopping the impulse/behavior that is disturbing our inner balance.[12]

People who have been "cheated on" have another whole set of emotional challenges, including letting go of hurt and being able to trust again. All of these issues are extremely challenging. But I think it's possible to get through them by relying on the Holy Word — and lots of intense prayer and reflection.

God sent His Prophets into the world to teach and enlighten man, to explain to him the mystery of the Power of the Holy Spirit, to enable him to reflect the light, and so in his turn, to be the source of guidance to others. The Heavenly Books, the Bible, the Qur'án, and the other Holy Writings have been given by God as guides into the paths of Divine virtue, love, justice and peace.

Therefore I say unto you that ye should strive to follow the counsels of these Blessed Books, and so order your lives that ye may, following the examples set before you, become yourselves the saints of the Most High!
— 'Abdu'l-Bahá
Paris Talks p. 61

How to Use This Book

This is not your typical compilation. Nor is it a standard workbook. It was designed to be read in sections, then contemplated – for an hour, a day or a week – before moving on to the next chapter. Each chapter does three things: It introduces a main idea with a quotation from the Bahá'í Writings, it reviews the main themes of the book with additional quotations and prayers, and it provides *Reflections* to help you focus more clearly on what you have read.

The chapter headings will tell you what the main idea is.

The repeating themes of the book include:

1. **The dangers of idle fancy and vain imaginings**
2. **Human nobility and our high station**
3. **Prayers for forgiveness**
4. **The importance of Fidelity and Faithfulness**
5. **Prayers of Praise and Thanksgiving**
6. **Laws, Obedience and the Fear of God**
7. **God's mercy**

These and some other themes will be repeated throughout the book, allowing you to consider them from different perspectives as your understanding deepens.

The *Reflections* are not Sacred Text. They are personal insights, gleaned from my own experience and through my years of work with people who have suffered from sexual abuse. Sometimes they are phrased as comments. Other times they are phrased as questions designed to draw attention to a particular phrase or idea in the quotations. Sometimes they include additional short quotations that support the main theme of the chapter.

These questions and observations reflect the insights that *I* got out of reading the Writings. If my comments do not apply to you, that is okay. They are simply jumping off points to help you find your own lessons in these Words of God.

I encourage you to take your time in reading this book. Bahá'u'lláh says *"One hour's reflection is preferable to seventy years of pious worship."* [13] This is particularly true when trying to unravel the challenges of such a difficult personal issue.

Use the white space — in the margins, between chapters and at the bottom of pages — to make notes and record thoughts and impressions that come to you.

This book can help — if you let it. It has helped me to write it, and I'm already turning to it on a daily basis for strength and guidance.

...in the beginning

one must make his steps firm in the Covenant

so that the confirmations of Bahá'u'lláh

may encircle from all sides,

the cohorts of the Supreme Concourse

may become the supporters and the helpers,

and the exhortations and

advices of 'Abdu'l-Bahá,

like unto the pictures engraved on stone,

may remain permanent and ineffaceable

in the tablets of the hearts.

— 'Abdu'l-Bahá

Meditation 1

Why we need the Teachings of the Prophets of God

The Teachings of the Prophets of God and the Fear of God Result in Righteousness

"There are some who imagine that an innate sense of human dignity will prevent man from committing evil actions and insure his spiritual and material perfection. That is, that an individual who is characterized with natural intelligence, high resolve, and a driving zeal, will, without any consideration for the severe punishments consequent on evil acts, or for the great rewards of righteousness, instinctively refrain from inflicting harm on his fellow men and will hunger and thirst to do good. And yet, if we ponder the lessons of history it will become evident that this very sense of honor and dignity is itself one of the bounties deriving from the instructions of the Prophets of God. We also observe in infants the signs of aggression and lawlessness, and that if a child is deprived of a teacher's instructions his undesirable qualities increase from one moment to the next. It is therefore clear that the emergence of this natural sense of human dignity and honor is the result of education. Secondly, even if we grant for the sake of the argument that instinctive intelligence and an innate moral quality would prevent wrongdoing, it is obvious that individuals so characterized are as rare as the philosopher's stone. An assumption of this sort cannot be validated by mere words, it must be supported by the facts. Let us see what power in creation impels the masses toward righteous aims and deeds!

Faithful

"Aside from this, if that rare individual who does exemplify such a faculty should also become an embodiment of the fear of God, it is certain that his strivings toward righteousness would be strongly reinforced."
— 'Abdu'l-Bahá [14]

Idle Fancies and Vain Imaginings

"Protect us, we beseech Thee, O my Lord, from the hosts of idle fancies and vain imaginations."
— Bahá'u'lláh [15]

My State

"My God, my Adored One, my King, my Desire! What tongue can voice my thanks to Thee? I was heedless, Thou didst awaken me. I had turned back from Thee, Thou didst graciously aid me to turn towards Thee. I was as one dead, Thou didst quicken me with the water of life. I was withered, Thou didst revive me with the heavenly stream of Thine utterance which hath flowed forth from the Pen of the All-Merciful." — Bahá'u'lláh [16]

Putting on the Characteristics of God, Obedience

"You say you wish your life to please Him. The way is simple but difficult. It is to learn the Commands of God as much as you can, and to live them. It is to seek the "pearl of great price," the Truth, to abandon all self-desires to attain one thing-THE LOVE OF GOD. The first act and evidence of that love is-obedience. Finding the Truth, receive it gladly, and live it. Not asceticism, not self-degradation, nor fleeing from earth's activities, but rather-all that which love to God and love to man implies, the cutting of the self from the lower loves of jealousy, envy, greed, and self-desires, and putting on the garments of love, patience, kindness, justice, mercy-the "Characteristics of God!"   — Thornton Chase [17]

Purity, the Door to Freedom

"Among the highest aspirations of all people is freedom. It is their dream, their expressed ideal, the object of their constant struggle. Yet, few in modern society recognize that purity is the door to freedom...."
— Paul Lample [18]

Prayer for Forgiveness and Pardon

"*By Thy sovereignty, O Thou Who art glorified in the hearts of men. I have turned to Thee, forsaking mine own will and desire, that Thy holy will and pleasure may rule within me and direct me according to that which the pen of Thy eternal decree hath destined for me. This servant, O Lord, though helpless turneth to the Orb of Thy Power, though abased hasteneth unto the Dayspring of Glory, though needy craveth the Ocean of Thy Grace. I beseech Thee by Thy favor and bounty, cast him not away. Thou art verily the Almighty, the Pardoner, the Compassionate.*" — Bahá'u'lláh [19]

Fidelity

"*We have forbidden you perfidious acts, and not that which will demonstrate fidelity. Have ye clung to the standards fixed by your own selves, and cast the standards of God behind your backs? Fear God, and be not of the foolish. But for man, who would make mention of Me on My earth, and how could My attributes and My name have been revealed?*" — Bahá'u'lláh [20]

God's Mercy

"*God hath forgiven what is past. Henceforward everyone should utter that which is meet and seemly, and should refrain from slander, abuse and whatever causeth sadness in men.*" — Bahá'u'lláh [21]

Faithful

The Station of Man
"The station of man is great, very great. God has created man after His own image and likeness. He has endowed him with a mighty power which is capable of discovering the mysteries of phenomena. Through its use man is able to arrive at ideal conclusions instead of being restricted to the mere plane of sense impressions. As he possesses sense endowment in common with the animals, it is evident that he is distinguished above them by his conscious power of penetrating abstract realities. He acquires divine wisdom; he searches out the mysteries of creation; he witnesses the radiance of omnipotence; he attains the second birth – that is to say, he is born out of the material world just as he is born of the mother; he attains to everlasting life; he draws nearer to God; his heart is replete with the love of God. This is the foundation of the world of humanity; this is the image and likeness of God; this is the reality of man; otherwise, he is an animal. Verily, God has created the animal in the image and likeness of man, for though man outwardly is human, yet in nature he possesses animal tendencies." '   — Abdu'l-Bahá [22]

Nobility
"O Lord, my God! This is a child that hath sprung from the loins of one of Thy servants to whom Thou has granted a distinguished station in the Tablets of Thine irrevocable decree in the Books of Thy behest."
— Bahá'u'lláh [23]

"Thou didst bring mankind into being to know Thee and to serve Thy Cause, that their station might thereby be uplifted by virtue of the things Thou hast revealed in Thy Scriptures, Thy Books, and Thy Tablets."
— Bahá'u'lláh [24]

Praise and Thanksgiving
   "O my God! O my God! I yield Thee thanks that Thou hast directed me towards Thyself, hast guided me unto Thy horizon, hast clearly set forth for me Thy Path, hast revealed to me Thy testimony and enabled me to set my face towards Thee...
   "Blessing be unto Thee, O Lord of Names and glory be unto Thee, O Creator of the heavens, inasmuch as Thou hast through the power of Thy Name, the Self-Subsisting, given me to drink of Thy sealed wine, and hast caused me to draw nigh unto Thee and hast enabled me to recognize the Dayspring of Thine utterance, the Manifestation of Thy signs, the Fountainhead of Thy laws and commandments and the Source of Thy wisdom and bestowals."   — Bahá'u'lláh [25]

   "In short, O ye friends of God and maidservants of the Merciful! The hand of divine bounty hath placed upon your heads a tranquil crown, the precious gems of which shall shine eternally over all regions. Appreciate this bounty, loose your tongues in praise and thanksgiving, and engage in the promulgation of the divine teachings, for this is the spirit of life and the means of salvation."
                                  — 'Abdu'l-Bahá [26]

— *Notes* —

The Law of the Lord (From the Bible)
 "The law of the Lord is perfect, reviving the soul; the testimony of the Lord is sure, making wise the simple; the precepts of the Lord are right, rejoicing the heart; the commandment of the Lord is pure, enlightening the eyes; the fear of the Lord is clean, enduring forever; the ordinances of the Lord are true, and righteous altogether. More to be desired are they than gold even much fine gold; sweeter also than honey and drippings of the honeycomb. Moreover by them is thy servant warned; in keeping them there is great reward. But who can discern his errors? Clear thou me from hidden faults. Keep back thy servant also from presumptuous sins; let them not have dominion over me! Then I shall be blameless, and innocent of great transgressions. Let the words of my mouth and the meditation of my heart be acceptable in thy sight, O Lord my rock and my redeemer."
— Psalms [27]

 "Oh, how I love Thy Law! It is my meditation all the day. Thy commandment makes me wiser than my enemies, for it is ever with me. I have more understanding than all my teachers, for thy testimonies are my meditation. I understand more than the aged for I keep Thy precepts. I hold back my feet from every evil way in order to keep Thy word. Through Thy precepts I get understanding; therefore I hate every false way."
— Psalms [28]

 "Fear God, and keep his commandments: for this is the whole duty of man." — Ecclesiastes [29]

Remaining

Reflection: Sometimes I shame myself mercilessly when I break a commandment of God. **I** know I can grow faster through being gentle with myself and truly BELIEVING in God's mercy and grace and my nobility. Since He is Merciful and expects me to be merciful to others, then it makes sense that I HAVE to be self-merciful in order to please Him since I am His creation and He loves His creation. What would make me believe Bahá'u'lláh when He says I am created noble?

Reflection: The subject of shame plays a major part in the Bahá'í Writings and reflections. Of course, it is an emotion that is sometimes in our society considered completely unnecessary and uncalled for, but the Bahá'í Writings say otherwise, such as: *"The fear of God hath ever been the prime factor in the education of His creatures. Well is it with them that have attained thereunto!"* Many individuals have the opposite problem of excessive shame and "self-loathing," as I offer here. Offering a spiritual, wise and moderate approach to one's sense of shame is an important element of this book, without either denying the value and constructive force of the sense of shame or indulging in it to the point of paralysis. It is important to convey that both allowing oneself to experience shame and believing in one's nobility and in God's grace and forgiveness go together; they are not alternatives. I raise this simply to highlight its importance and the potential for more explicitly developing this sensitive balance throughout the work.

– Notes –

Reflection: Can I repent without self-loathing? What is required to repent without self-loathing? Avoiding certain behavior, whether married or not, requires a noble commitment. Why would Bahá'u'lláh teach me to pray, **"My great confidence** in Thy bounty, however, reviveth my hope in Thee and **my certitude** that Thou wilt bountifully deal with me emboldeneth me to extol Thee, and to ask of Thee the things Thou dost possess..." if He did not want to emphasize **my NOBILITY in repentance?**

Reflection: Do I KNOW what I am praying? If I only knew and recognized every word that passes over my lips, I would be transformed as I read these prayers! I would realize that my NOBILITY has been irrevocable decreed by God as implied in the prayer for children above! It's a foregone conclusion!

Reflection: At the point where I become mindful of my disobedience, it may be because I truly feel sorrow that I have hurt someone dear to me; it may be because I have been stuck, and a change has come over me as a result of prayer. I may realize that I have been put through a series of lessons to awaken me. That is the moment where the burden will be lifted and I am free of the prison of self. The natural response is to PRAISE God and thank Him for removing my idle fancies and vain imaginings, for lifting the burden and restoring and confirming my nobility. Quotations for praising God will be a part of the series of reflections in each chapter of this meditative book.

— *Notes* —

Meditation 2

Me?
A Saint who could subdue the cities of men's hearts?

The Fear of God

"*O friends, help the Oppressed One with well-pleasing virtues and good deeds! Today let every soul desire to attain the highest station. He must not regard what is in him, but what is in God. It is not for him to regard what shall advantage himself, but that whereby the Word of God which must be obeyed shall be upraised. The heart must be sanctified from every form of selfishness and lust, for the weapons of the tranquil and the saints were and are the fear of God. That is the buckler which guardeth man from the arrows of hatred and abomination. Unceasingly hath the standard of piety been victorious, and accounted amongst the most puissant hosts of the world. Thereby do the saints subdue the cities of [men's] hearts by the permission of God, the Lord of hosts. Darkness hath encompassed the earth: the lamp which giveth light was and is wisdom. The dictates thereof must be observed under all circumstances. And of wisdom is the regard of place and the utterance of discourse according to measure and state. And of wisdom is decision; for man should not accept whatsoever anyone sayeth.*" — 'Abdu'l-Bahá [31]

Idle Fancies and Vain Imaginings

"Well is it with him who, aided by the living waters of the utterance of Him Who is the Desire of all men, hath purified himself from idle fancies and vain imaginings, and torn away, in the name of the All-Possessing, the Most High, the veils of doubt, and renounced the world and all that is therein, and directed himself towards the Most Great Prison."   — Bahá'u'lláh [30]

Human Nature Made Up of Possibilities for Both Good and Evil

"... First concerning the human soul and its nature. According to the Bahá'í conception, the soul of man, or in other words his inner spiritual self or reality, is not dualistic. There is no such thing, as the Zoroastrians believe, as a double reality in man, a definite higher self and lower self. The latter is capable of development in either way. All depends fundamentally on the training or education which man receives. Human nature is made up of possibilities for both good and evil. True religion can enable it to soar in the highest realm of the spirit, while its absence can, as we already witness around us, cause it to fall to the lowest depth of degradation and misery."   — Shoghi Effendi [32]

The Station of Man

"In brief, the purport is this: The teachings of Bahá'u'lláh are boundless, innumerable; time will not allow us to mention them in detail. The foundation of progress and real prosperity in the human world is reality, for reality is the divine standard and the bestowal of God. Reality is reasonableness, and reasonableness is ever conducive to the honorable station of man. Reality is the guidance of God. Reality is the cause of illumination of mankind. Reality is love, ever working for the welfare of humanity. Reality is the bond which conjoins hearts. This ever uplifts man toward higher stages of progress and attainment. Reality is the unity of mankind, conferring everlasting life. Reality is perfect equality, the foundation of agreement between the nations, the first step toward international peace."

— 'Abdu'l-Bahá [33]

Praise and Thanksgiving

"It is true that every one of God's servants, and in particular those who are on fire with the Faith, have been allotted this task of servitude to Almighty God; still, the duty imposed upon us is greater than that which hath been laid upon the rest. To Him do we look for grace and favour and strength.

"All praise and thanksgiving be unto the Blessed Beauty, for calling into action the armies of His Abha Kingdom, and sending forth to us His never-interrupted aid, dependable as the rising stars." — 'Abdu'l-Bahá [34]

Prayer of Thankfulness

"O compassionate God! Thanks be to Thee for Thou hast awakened me and made me conscious. Thou hast given me a seeing eye and favored me with a hearing ear, hast led me to Thy kingdom and guided me to Thy path. Thou hast shown me the right way and caused me to enter the ark of deliverance. O God! Keep me steadfast and make me firm and staunch. Protect me from violent tests and preserve me in the strongly fortified fortress of Thy Covenant and Testament. Thou art the Powerful. Thou art the Seeing. Thou art the Hearing."

— 'Abdu'l-Bahá [35]

Reflection: What is the difference between "self-degradation" and humbling myself and accepting correction out of wisdom because of "the fear of God," which is a light in the darkness? If I think of "the fear of God" as a weapon against lust and abomination, how is this different than self-punishment?

Reflection: At first thought I may not believe I could become a "saint" because I know the secret thoughts I have, but I also know that I want to do everything I can to have a wholesome character. What successes have I had during my journey through life? Is that success repeatable? How could I repeat such a victory now? Do I have relationships in which I need to set clear boundaries?

Reflection: What verses in the Revelation of Bahá'u'lláh really encourage me to believe I can "soar in the highest realm of the spirit?" How do the Writings of Bahá'u'lláh lift me up toward higher stages of progress and attainment?

Reflection: If reality is the cause of my illumination, love, and unity, what is the fruit of idle fancies and vain imaginings? Can I monitor myself through the day and catch myself when thinking in idle fancies and vain imaginings about men or women other than my spouse? That is nobility in action! If I am thinking thoughts of self-punishment, those are also idle fancies and vain imaginings! When I bring myself to account each day, I can also look at the good things I have done and praise myself for the effort I put into creating a new foundation for my thinking that is based on the Revelation of Bahá'u'lláh!

Meditation 3

Support for the Natural Human Condition

Idle Fancies and Vain imaginings
"By the righteousness of God! Idle fancies have debarred men from the Horizon of Certitude, and vain imaginings withheld them from the Choice Sealed Wine."
— Bahá'u'lláh [36]

Desire and Passion
"Desire and passion, like two unmanageable horses, have wrested the reins of control from him and are galloping madly in the wilderness. This is the cause of the degradation of the world of humanity. This is the cause of its retrogression into the appetites and passions of the animal kingdom. Instead of divine advancement we find sensual captivity and debasement of heavenly virtues of the soul. By devotion to the carnal, mortal world human susceptibilities sink to the level of animalism."
— 'Abdu'l-Bahá [37]

Prayer for Forgiveness
"He is the Mighty, the Pardoner, the Compassionate! O God, my God! Thou beholdest Thy servants in the abyss of perdition and error; where is Thy light of divine guidance, O Thou the Desire of the world? Thou knowest their helplessness and their feebleness; where is Thy power, O Thou in Whose grasp lie the powers of heaven and earth?

"Decree for me, by Thy bounty, O Lord, that which shall prosper me in this world and hereafter and shall draw me nigh unto Thee, O Thou Who art the Lord of all men. There is none other God but Thee, the One, the Mighty, the Glorified."
— Bahá'u'lláh [38]

Fidelity

"Adorn your heads with the garlands of trustworthiness and fidelity, your hearts with the attire of the Fear of God, your tongues with absolute truthfulness, your bodies with the vesture of courtesy." — Bahá'u'lláh [39]

The Station of Man

"The purpose underlying the revelation of every heavenly Book, nay, of every divinely-revealed verse, is to endue all men with righteousness and understanding, so that peace and tranquility may be firmly established amongst them. Whatsoever instilleth assurance into the hearts of men, whatsoever exalteth their station or promoteth their contentment, is acceptable in the sight of God. How lofty is the station which man, if he but choose to fulfill his high destiny, can attain! To what depths of degradation he can sink, depths which the meanest of creatures have never reached! Seize, O friends, the chance which this Day offereth you, and deprive not yourselves of the liberal effusions of His grace. I beseech God that He may graciously enable every one of you to adorn himself, in this blessed Day, with the ornament of pure and holy deeds. He, verily, doeth whatsoever He willeth." — Bahá'u'lláh [40]

Praise and Thanksgiving

"O LORD, my God! Praise and thanksgiving be unto Thee for Thou hast guided me to the highway of the kingdom, suffered me to walk in this straight and far-stretching path, illumined my eye by beholding the splendors of Thy light, inclined my ear to the melodies of the birds of holiness from the kingdom of mysteries and attracted my heart with Thy love among the righteous."

 — 'Abdu'l-Bahá [41]

Reflection: When do I start to lose my grip on my daily worship? What is it that keeps me from praying... time?...lack of energy?...the busyness of life in general?...lack of motivation...depression? The Choice Sealed Wine is free to me everyday of my life, but the moment I stop drinking I enter a wilderness of idle fancies. That's why 'Abdu'l-Bahá says man is always in danger.[42] He knows my helplessness and feebleness. It's part of the human condition. *"For the days of a man are full of peril and he cannot rely on so much as a moment more of life..."* 'Abdu'l-Baha [31]

Reflection: Have I ever experienced "peace and tranquility" in the community of the friends?[43] What instilled "assurance in my heart" at that moment? What test didn't I see that interrupted that contentment? How can I get back on the "straight and far-stretching path?" What would make me be gentle with myself and BELIEVE in God's mercy and forgiveness?

– Notes –

— *Notes* —

Meditation 4

What Maintains the Order of the World?

Idle Fancies and Vain Imaginings

"We have forbidden men to walk after the imaginations of their hearts, that they may be enabled to recognize Him Who is the sovereign Source and Object of all knowledge, and may acknowledge whatsoever He may be pleased to reveal. Witness how they have entangled themselves with their idle fancies and vain imaginations. By My life! They are themselves the victims of what their own hearts have devised, and yet they perceive it not. Vain and profitless is the talk of their lips, and yet they understand not.

"We beseech God that He may graciously vouchsafe His grace unto all men, and enable them to attain the knowledge of Him and of themselves. By My life! Whoso hath known Him shall soar in the immensity of His love, and shall be detached from the world and all that is therein. Nothing on earth shall deflect him from his course, how much less they who, prompted by their vain imaginations, speak those things which God hath forbidden." — Bahá'u'lláh [44]

Evil Passions and Corrupt Desires

"They whom God hath endued with insight will readily recognize that the precepts laid down by God constitute the highest means for the maintenance of order in the world and the security of its peoples. He that turneth away from them is accounted among the abject and foolish. We, verily, have commanded you to refuse the dictates of your evil passions and corrupt desires, and not to transgress the bounds which the Pen of the Most High hath fixed, for these are the breath of life unto all created things. The seas of Divine wisdom and Divine utterance have risen under the breath of the breeze of the All-Merciful. Hasten to drink your fill, O men of understanding! They that have violated the Covenant of God by breaking His commandments, and have turned back on their heels, these have erred grievously in the sight of God, the All-Possessing, the Most High."

— Bahá'u'lláh [45]

Fidelity

"Should any one of you enter a city, he should become a centre of attraction by reason of his sincerity, his faithfulness and love, his honesty and fidelity, his truthfulness and loving-kindness towards all the peoples of the world, so that the people of that city may cry out and say: 'This man is unquestionably a Bahá'í, for his manners, his behaviour, his conduct, his morals, his nature, and disposition reflect the attributes of the Bahá'ís.' Not until ye attain this station can ye be said to have been faithful to the Covenant and Testament of God. For He hath, through irrefutable Texts, entered into a binding Covenant with us all, requiring us to act in accordance with His sacred instructions and counsels."

— 'Abdu'l-Bahá [46]

Prayer for Forgiveness and Protection

"Attire, O my Lord, both my inner and outer being with the raiment of Thy favors and Thy Loving kindness. Keep me safe, then, from whatsoever may be abhorrent unto Thee, and graciously assist me and my kindred to obey Thee and to shun whatsoever may stir up any evil or corrupt desire within me.

"Thou, truly, art the Lord of all mankind, and the Possessor of this world and of the next. No God is there save Thee, the All-Knowing, All-Wise." — Bahá'u'lláh [47]

The Station of Man

"Be ye warned, O men of understanding. It ill beseemeth the station of man to commit tyranny; rather it behoveth him to observe equity and be attired with the raiment of justice under all conditions. Beseech ye the One true God that He may, through the power of the hand of loving-kindness and spiritual education, purge and purify certain souls from the defilement of evil passions and corrupt desires, that they may arise and unloose their tongues for the sake of God, that perchance the evidences of injustice may be blotted out and the splendour of the light of justice may shed its radiance upon the whole world. The people are ignorant, and they stand in need of those who will expound the truth."
— Bahá'u'lláh [48]

Praise and Thanksgiving

"Therefore, we must endeavor always, cry, supplicate and invoke the Kingdom of God to grant us full capacity in order that the bestowals of God may become revealed and manifest in us. And as we attain to these heavenly bounties, we shall offer thanks unto the threshold of oneness. Then shall we rejoice in the Lord that in this wonderful century and glorious age, under the shelter of the Kingdom of God we have enjoyed these bestowals and will arise in praise and thanksgiving. Therefore, I first exhort myself and then I entreat you to appreciate this great bestowal, recognize this most great guidance, accept these bounties of the Lord. You must endeavor day and night to become worthy of a generous portion of these gifts and realize full capacity of attainment. Praise be to God!" — 'Abdu'l-Bahá [49]

Reflection: Boundaries and limits, the commandments of God, are good for me psychologically. They assure me of security and are the means for *"the maintenance of order in the world."* What are the veils that keep me from seeing the logic of this insight and cause my descent into *"evil passions and corrupt desires?"* Acting out sexually can be caused by being abused as a child and should be treated by a therapist. It indicates that the individual needs to learn how to set boundaries for themselves and respect the boundaries of others.[50]

Reflection: The act of adultery is a form of tyranny. It is destructive of the covenant between two people who are married to one another. It is an injustice to the children of that union. If I beseech God in prayer with great urgency, He tells me he will purge and purify my soul from defilement. He will attract me by His mercifulness.[51] Remember, the difference between material civilization and Divine Civilization is that one trains by force, the other by spiritualization and love.[52]

– Notes –

Meditation 5

Through the Holy Spirit We shall become the Light of the World

Idle Fancies and Vain Imaginings

"Arise, O people, and, by the power of God's might, resolve to gain the victory over your own selves, that haply the whole earth may be freed and sanctified from its servitude to the gods of its idle fancies – gods that have inflicted such loss upon, and are responsible for the misery of, their wretched worshipers."

— Bahá'u'lláh [53]

A Dove of Heaven or a Captive of Self and Passion

"How debased is such a nature! God has created man in order that he may be a dove of the Kingdom, a heavenly candle, a recipient of eternal life. God has created man in order that he may be resuscitated through the breaths of the Holy Spirit and become the light of the world. How debased the soul which can find enjoyment in this darkness, occupied with itself, the captive of self and passion, wallowing in the mire of the material world! How degraded is such a nature! What an ignorance this is! What a blindness! How glorious the station of man who has partaken of the heavenly food and built the temple of his everlasting residence in the world of heaven!

"The Manifestations of God have come into the world to free man from these bonds and chains of the world of nature. Although They walked upon the earth, They lived in heaven. They were not concerned about material sustenance and prosperity of this world. Their bodies were subjected to inconceivable distress, but Their spirits ever

soared in the highest realms of ecstasy. The purpose of Their coming, Their teaching and suffering was the freedom of man from himself. Shall we, therefore, follow in Their footsteps, escape from this cage of the body or continue subject to its tyranny? Shall we pursue the phantom of a mortal happiness which does not exist or turn toward the tree of life and the joys of its eternal fruits?" — 'Abdu'l-Bahá [54]

Fidelity

"It behoveth thee, however, to exert thine utmost to attain the very essence of fidelity. This implieth to be well assured in thy heart and to testify with thy tongue." — Bahá'u'lláh [55]

Prayer for Forgiveness and Pardon

"O Lord! We are sinners, but Thou art the Forgiver. We are submerged in the ocean of shortcomings, but Thou art the Pardoner, the Kind. Forgive our sins and bless us with Thine abundant grace. Grant us the privilege of beholding Thy Countenance, and give us the chalice of joy and bliss. We are captives of our own transgressions, and Thou art the King of bountiful favors. We are drowned in a sea of iniquities and Thou art the Lord of infinite mercy. Thou art the Giver, the Glorious, the Eternal, the Bounteous; and Thou art the All-Gracious, the All-Merciful, the Omnipotent, He Who is the Bestower of gifts and the Forgiver of sins. Verily, Thou art He to Whom we turn for the remission of our failings, He Who is the Lord of lords." — 'Abdu'l-Bahá [56]

The Station of Man

"The All-Merciful hath conferred upon man the faculty of vision, and endowed him with the power of hearing. Some have described him as the "lesser world," when, in reality, he should be regarded as the "greater world." The potentialities inherent in the station of man, the full measure of his destiny on earth, the innate excellence of his reality, must all be manifested in this promised Day of God." — Bahá'u'lláh [57]

Praise and Thanksgiving

"Praise and thanksgiving be unto Providence that out of all the realities in existence He has chosen the reality of man and has honored it with intellect and wisdom, the two most luminous lights in either world. Through the agency of this great endowment, He has in every epoch cast on the mirror of creation new and wonderful configurations. If we look objectively upon the world of being, it will become apparent that from age to age, the temple of existence has continually been embellished with a fresh grace, and distinguished with an ever-varying splendor, deriving from wisdom and the power of thought." — 'Abdu'l-Bahá [58]

– Notes –

Reflection: Bahá'u'lláh wants me to stay close to my community and His Writings so that I might be "freed from servitude" to my idle fancies, and be a light shining in the world. How can I stay closer to my community and Bahá'u'lláh's Revelation? What is in my culture that grabs my attention, preoccupies my mind, feeds my idle fancies, and keeps me from being a "dove of the Kingdom"?

Reflection: Is a person home free when he or she reads and accepts that the *"Manifestations of God have come to free man from the bonds of nature"*? What else is required of me in order that I may be tranquil *"through the breaths of the Holy Spirit"*? Am I pursuing a phantom of happiness when I succumb to temptation? Isn't it just the repetition of a pattern?...An excitement that ends in disillusionment?....An addiction born in fantasy?

Reflection: Those who are humble servants know that but for the mercy of God, he or she is captive of their own transgressions. When I approach God with honesty in prayer, He will show me grace and forgive my sins. Doesn't God know all about my idle fancies and wayward actions? Why then, like Abdul-Bahá, do we need to pray for mercy regarding our sins? What are the inherent potentialities of my reality should I repent and pray sincerely for forgiveness?

Reflection: The power of discernment is essential for us to develop. When we have the power of discernment, we can discern right from wrong. God is patient while we are developing this power. He cannot give it to us outright...it is something we have to develop through our own senses, understanding of God's word and volition. Bahá'u'lláh taught directly through "contrast" so that His followers could develop discernment regarding who was a true believe and who was not.[59]

Meditation 6

Baháʼu'lláh has Claimed the Hearts of Mankind as His Own

Idle Fancies and Vain Imaginings

"We have forbidden men to walk after the imaginations of their hearts, that they may be enabled to recognize Him Who is the sovereign Source and Object of all knowledge, and may acknowledge whatsoever He may be pleased to reveal. Witness how they have entangled themselves with their idle fancies and vain imaginations. By My life! They are themselves the victims of what their own hearts have devised, and yet they perceive it not. Vain and profitless is the talk of their lips, and yet they understand not." — Baháʼu'lláh [60]

"...[M]an's supreme honor and real happiness lie in self-respect, in high resolves and noble purposes, in integrity and moral quality, in immaculacy of mind."
— ʻAbdu'l-Bahá [61]

The Fear of God

"Again, there are those famed and accomplished men of learning, possessed of praiseworthy qualities and vast erudition, who lay hold on the strong handle of the fear of God and keep to the ways of salvation."
— ʻAbdu'l-Bahá [62]

Self as Identity or Self as Ego

"Regarding the questions you asked: Self has really two meanings, or is used in two senses, in the Baháʼí writings; one is self, the identity of the individual created by God. This is the self mentioned in such passages as 'he hath known God who hath known himself etc.'. The other self is the ego, the dark, animalistic heritage each one of us has, the lower nature that can develop into a monster of selfishness, brutality, lust and so on. It is this self we must struggle against, or this side of our natures, in order to strengthen and free the spirit within us and help it to attain perfection."

"Self-sacrifice means to subordinate this lower nature and its desires to the more godly and noble side of ourselves. Ultimately, in its highest sense, self-sacrifice means to give our will and our all to God to do with as He pleases. Then He purifies and glorifies our true self until it becomes a shining and wonderful reality."

— *Shoghi Effendi* [63]

Piety and a Saintly Character

"The purpose of the one true God in manifesting Himself is to summon all mankind to truthfulness and sincerity, to piety and trustworthiness, to resignation and submissiveness to the Will of God, to forbearance and kindliness, to uprightness and wisdom. His object is to array every man with the mantle of a saintly character, and to adorn him with the ornament of holy and goodly deeds.

"Say: Have mercy on yourselves and on your fellowmen, and suffer not the Cause of God – a Cause which is immeasurably exalted above the inmost essence of sanctity – to be sullied with the stain of your idle fancies, your unseemly and corrupt imaginations."

— *Bahá'u'lláh* [64]

"Thy generous Lord will...forgive thy sins and transform them into goodly deeds." — *'Abdu'l-Bahá* [65]

Prayer for Protection
"O Thou kind Lord! We are servants of Thy Threshold, taking shelter at Thy holy Door. We seek no refuge save only this strong pillar, turn nowhere for a haven but unto Thy safekeeping. Protect us, bless us, support us, make us such that we shall love but Thy good pleasure, utter only Thy praise, follow only the pathway of truth, that we may become rich enough to dispense with all save Thee, and receive our gifts from the sea of Thy beneficence, that we may ever strive to exalt Thy Cause and to spread Thy sweet savors far and wide, that we may become oblivious of self and occupied only with Thee, and disown all else and be caught up in Thee.

"O Thou Provider, O Thou Forgiver! Grant us Thy grace and loving-kindness, Thy gifts and Thy bestowals, and sustain us, that we may attain our goal. Thou art the Powerful, the Able, the Knower, the Seer; and, verily, Thou art the Generous, and, verily, Thou art the All-Merciful, and, verily, Thou art the Ever-Forgiving, He to Whom repentance is due, He Who forgiveth even the most grievous of sins." — 'Abdu'l-Bahá [66]

The Station of Man
"Were man to appreciate the greatness of his station and the loftiness of his destiny he would manifest naught save goodly character, pure deeds, and a seemly and praiseworthy conduct." — Bahá'u'lláh [67]

Praise and Thanksgiving
"But that which God (glorious is His mention) hath desired for Himself is the hearts of His servants, which are treasures of praise and love of the Lord and stores of divine knowledge and wisdom." — 'Abdu'l-Bahá [68]

Faithful

Reflection: Bahá'u'lláh calls me to be responsible for what my own heart contains. How can I release myself from the grip of idle fancies, vain imaginations, romantic notions, and physical attractions? How can I release myself from a pattern set long ago of being a victim, a perpetrator, a hedonist, a pleasure-seeking creature, a foolish romantic who loses self in romance? Would I need to seek the help of a therapist, the help of my Local Spiritual Assembly? If only I could believe that there is no shame in asking for help regarding my secret thoughts and life. If I rely upon the Word of God to guide me, I believe I can.

Reflection: There are people in the Bahá'í community who have been courageous enough to subordinate their will "to God to do with as He pleases." Wonderful stories of reconstructed lives. I have to be willing to trust and find a new way of relating to those who either victimize me, violate my boundaries or encourage my lower nature. Is my way of relating to others working for me? Where are my patterns of behavior against the Will of God? How do I give my will and my all to God to do with as He pleases"? Have I done this in the past? Could I do it now? Have I ever had the experience of reflecting on an improvement of my behavior and realized that God brought me to that place? *"All things feareth him who fears God!"Baha'u'llah*[69] *"He who puts his trust in God, God will suffice him"* and *"He who fears God, God will send him relief." Bahá'u'lláh* [70]

Reflection: I would only thank God for the grain of wisdom embedded in my heart, and beg for a more fertile heart. *"If it be Thy pleasure, make me to grow as a tender herb in the meadows of Thy grace, that the gentle winds of Thy will may stir me up and bend me into conformity with Thy pleasure, in such wise that my movement and my stillness may be wholly directed by Thee."* Bahá'u'lláh [71]

There is no need for me to compare myself to others. I have access to my fair share of the grace of God. There is no soul who is so lofty that they are not challenged by their own imperfections. I can be thankful for my progress so far, and humbly pray that it will continue.

— *Notes* —

- *Notes* -

Meditation 7

The Importance of Fidelity

Idle Fancies and Vain Imaginings

"O My servants! Let not your vain hopes and idle fancies sap the foundations of your belief in the All-Glorious God, inasmuch as such imaginings have been wholly unprofitable unto men, and failed to direct their steps unto the straight Path. Think ye, O My servants, that the Hand of My all-encompassing, My overshadowing, and transcendent sovereignty is chained up, that the flow of Mine ancient, My ceaseless, and all-pervasive mercy is checked, or that the clouds of My sublime and unsurpassed favors have ceased to rain their gifts upon men? Can ye imagine that the wondrous works that have proclaimed My divine and resistless power are withdrawn, or that the potency of My will and purpose hath been deterred from directing the destinies of mankind?"

— Bahá'u'lláh [72]

The Fear of God

"Those eminent divines and men of learning who walk the straight pathway and are versed in the secrets of divine wisdom and informed of the inner realities of the sacred Books; who wear in their hearts the jewel of the fear of God, and whose luminous faces shine with the lights of salvation – these are alert to the present need and they understand the requirements of modern times, and certainly devote all their energies toward encouraging the advancement of learning and civilization. "Are they equal, those who know, and those who do not know?... Or is the darkness equal with the light?"

— 'Abdu'l-Bahá [73]

Faithful 41

Hold Fast to the Statutes, Ordinances and Commandments of God

"These are the ordinances of God that have been set down in the Books and Tablets by His Most Exalted Pen. Hold ye fast unto His statutes and commandments, and be not of those who, following their own idle fancies and vain imaginings, have clung to the standards fixed by their own selves, and cast behind their backs the standards laid down by God." — Bahá'u'lláh [74]

Fidelity

"Indeed thy Lord loveth fidelity as found in the realm of creation, and He hath given it precedence over most of the praiseworthy qualities. Verily, He is Potent and Powerful." — Bahá'u'lláh [75]

Prayer for Forgiveness

"I am a sinner, O my Lord, and Thou art the Ever-Forgiving. As soon as I recognized Thee, I hastened to attain the exalted court of Thy loving-kindness. Forgive me, O my Lord, my sins which have hindered me from walking in the ways of Thy good pleasure, and from attaining the shores of the ocean of Thy oneness.

"There is no one, O my Lord, who can deal bountifully with me to whom I can turn my face, and none who can have compassion on me that I may crave his mercy. Cast me not out, I implore Thee of the presence of Thy grace, neither do Thou withhold from me the outpourings of Thy generosity and bounty." — Bahá'u'lláh [76]

The Station of Man

"Great is the station of man. Great must also be his endeavours for the rehabilitation of the world and the well-being of nations. I beseech the One true God to graciously confirm thee in that which beseemeth man's station." — Bahá'u'lláh [77]

Praise and Thanksgiving

"Through the revelation of Thy grace, O Lord, Thou didst call Me into being on a night such as this, and lo, I am now lonely and forsaken in a mountain. Praise and thanksgiving be unto Thee for whatever conformeth to Thy pleasure within the empire of heaven and earth. And all sovereignty is Thine, extending beyond the uttermost range of the kingdoms of Revelation and Creation." — The Báb [78]

Reflection: What is the meaning of the Báb's prayer, *"All are His servants and all abide by His bidding?"* It is only when I am living out my idle fancies and vain imaginings that God's "divine and resistless power" SEEM to be withdrawn, but nothing can check His all-pervasive mercy. How can I mirror His Revelation instead of the world? How could I mirror the qualities and return to the fervency that uplifted me when I first joined this wonderful Cause which promised a blueprint for regenerating the world?

Reflection: What are my thoughts on the idea that by rehabilitating my own life and character, I participate in the rehabilitation of the world? 'Abdu'l-Bahá writes so gently and poetically about the effect I can have in this quotation: *"Make ready thy soul that thou mayest be like the light which shineth forth from the loftiest heights on the coast, by means of which guidance may be given to the timid ships amid the darkness of fog..."* [79]

Reflection: I think that *"He hath given it [fidelity] precedence over most of the praiseworthy qualities"* because it encompasses more than infidelity in marriage. It encompasses our faithfulness to Bahá'u'lláh, the Bahá'í Writings, willingness to sacrifice, the faithfulness to the Covenant and more. It is holding fast to His statutes and commandments, and our ultimate constancy and steadfastness to the Cause of God. Can I identify the ways that I show fidelity in my life and toward others?

Meditation 8

Don't be Shaken by the Tumult of Tests

Idle Fancies and Vain Imaginings
"Praised be Thou, O Lord my God! I implore Thee by Them Who are the Tabernacles of Thy Divine holiness, Who are the Manifestations of Thy transcendent unity and the Day-Springs of Thine inspiration and revelation, to grant that Thy servants may not be kept back from this Divine Law which, at Thy will and according to Thy pleasure, hath branched out from Thy most great Ocean. Do Thou, then, ordain for them that which Thou didst ordain for Thy chosen ones and for the righteous among Thy creatures, whose constancy in Thy Cause the tempests of trials have failed to shake, and whom the tumults of tests have been powerless to hinder from magnifying Thy most exalted Word – the Word through Which the heavens of men's idle fancies and vain imaginations have been split asunder. Thou art, verily, the Almighty, the All-Glorious, the All-Knowing." — Bahá'u'lláh [80]

The Fear of God
"For every thing, however, God has created a sign and symbol, and established standards and tests by which it may be known. The spiritually learned must be characterized by both inward and outward perfections; they must possess a good character, an enlightened nature, a pure intent, as well as intellectual power, brilliance and discernment, intuition, discretion and foresight, temperance, reverence, and a heartfelt fear of God."
— 'Abdu'l-Bahá [81]

Faithful

Freedom from Carnal Passions: The Holy Spirit

"Man cannot free himself from the rage of the carnal passions except by the help of the Holy Spirit. That is why He says baptism with the spirit, with water and with fire is necessary, and that it is essential – that is to say, the spirit of divine bounty, the water of knowledge and life, and the fire of the love of God. Man must be baptized with this spirit, this water and this fire so as to become filled with the eternal bounty. Otherwise, what is the use of baptizing with material water? No, this baptism with water was a symbol of repentance, and of seeking forgiveness of sins. But in the cycle of Bahá'u'lláh there is no longer need of this symbol; for its reality, which is to be baptized with the spirit and love of God, is understood and established."

—'Abdu'l-Bahá [82]

Returning to God's Mercy

"They that follow their lusts and corrupt inclinations, have erred and dissipated their efforts. They, indeed, are of the lost. Strive, O people, that your eyes may be directed towards the mercy of God, that your hearts may be attuned to His wondrous remembrance, that your souls may rest confidently upon His grace and bounty, that your feet may tread the path of His good-pleasure. Such are the counsels which I bequeath unto you. Would that ye might follow My counsels!"   — Bahá'u'lláh [83]

Prayer for Forgiveness and Mercy

"I am he, O my Lord, that hath set his face towards Thee, and fixed his hope on the wonders of Thy grace and the revelations of Thy bounty. I pray Thee that Thou wilt not suffer me to turn away disappointed from the door of Thy mercy, nor abandon me to such of Thy creatures as have repudiated Thy Cause.

"I am, O my God, Thy servant and the son of Thy servant. I have recognized Thy truth in Thy days, and have directed my steps towards the shores of Thy oneness, confessing Thy singleness, acknowledging Thy unity, and hoping for Thy forgiveness and pardon. Powerful art Thou to do what Thou willest; no God is there beside Thee, the All-Glorious, the Ever-Forgiving."

— Bahá'u'lláh [84]

The Station of Man

"O My servants! Could ye apprehend with what wonders of My munificence and bounty I have willed to entrust your souls, ye would, of a truth, rid yourselves of attachment to all created things, and would gain a true knowledge of your own selves – a knowledge which is the same as the comprehension of Mine own Being. Ye would find yourselves independent of all else but Me, and would perceive, with your inner and outer eye, and as manifest as the revelation of My effulgent Name, the seas of My loving-kindness and bounty moving within you. Suffer not your idle fancies, your evil passions, your insincerity and blindness of heart to dim the luster, or stain the sanctity, of so lofty a station. Ye are even as the bird which soareth, with the full force of its mighty wings and with complete and joyous confidence, through the immensity of the heavens, until, impelled to satisfy its hunger, it turneth longingly to the water and clay of the earth below it, and, having been entrapped in the mesh of its desire, findeth itself impotent to resume its flight to the realms whence it came. Powerless to shake off the burden weighing on its sullied wings, that bird, hitherto an inmate of the heavens, is now forced to seek a dwelling-place upon the dust. Wherefore, O My servants, defile not your wings with the clay of waywardness and vain desires, and suffer them not to be stained with the dust of envy and hate, that ye may not be hindered from soaring in the heavens of My divine knowledge."

— Bahá'u'lláh [85]

Faithful

Praise and Thanksgiving

"O Lord! Provide for the speedy growth of the Tree of Thy divine Unity; water it then, O Lord, with the flowing waters of Thy good-pleasure, and cause it, before the revelations of Thy divine assurance, to yield such fruits as Thou desirest for Thy glorification and exaltation, Thy praise and thanksgiving, and to magnify Thy Name, to laud the oneness of Thine Essence and to offer adoration unto Thee, inasmuch as all this lieth within Thy grasp and in that of none other." — The Báb [86]

Reflection: How have my tests in life enlightened me? What lessons have I learned? What tests have I experienced that I have had certitude that they were given as a protection for me and for which I felt truly thankful? If God is closer than my life vein as the word of God says, I can imagine that He has prepared lessons for me to awaken me and the question becomes, "How much have I learned to this point; and what more needs to be learned, instead of condemnation?" These are merciful lessons that may bring us to our knees and feel like a calamity, but they are light in the darkness.

Reflection: When I have been caught in the grip of carnal passions, how did I come to turn to the Holy Spirit for knowledge and the love of God? Do I turn to the Word of God every day for this renewal by the Holy Spirit? Isn't it essential?

Reflection: Have I prayed for others who appear to be going down a path of delusion? Expressed my concern to them – without judgment or prying? Have I asked others to pray for me and my spiritual growth – without confessing?

Meditation 9

What do I give up to Cleave unto Righteousness?

Idle Fancies and Vain Imagination

"We have forbidden men to walk after the imaginations of their hearts, that they may be enabled to recognize Him Who is the sovereign Source and Object of all knowledge, and may acknowledge whatsoever He may be pleased to reveal. Witness how they have entangled themselves with their idle fancies and vain imaginations. By My life! They are themselves the victims of what their own hearts have devised, and yet they perceive it not. Vain and profitless is the talk of their lips, and yet they understand not." — Bahá'u'lláh [87]

The Fear of God

"Purify thou, first, thy soul with the waters of renunciation, and adorn thine head with the crown of the fear of God, and thy temple with the ornament of reliance upon Him." — Bahá'u'lláh [88]

Cleave Unto Righteousness

"Valiant acts will ensure the triumph of this Cause, and a saintly character will reinforce its power. Cleave unto righteousness, O people of Bahá! This, verily, is the commandment which this wronged One has given unto you, and the first choice of his unrestrained Will for every one of you." — Bahá'u'lláh [89]

Be Ashamed. Let Your Eyes be Opened!

"Say: Be ashamed, O ye that call yourselves the lovers of the Ancient Beauty! Be ye admonished by the tribulation He hath suffered, by the burden of anguish He hath carried for the sake of God. Let your eyes be opened. To what purpose hath He labored, if the manifold trials He hath endured are, in the end, to result in such contemptible professions, and such wretched conduct? Every robber, every worker of iniquity, hath, in the days prior to My Revelation, uttered these same words, and performed these same deeds." — Bahá'u'lláh [90]

Prayer for Forgiveness and Mercy

"Thou seest me, O my Lord, with my face turned towards the heaven of Thy bounty and the ocean of Thy favor, withdrawn from all else beside Thee. I ask of Thee, by the splendors of the Sun of Thy revelation on Sinai, and the effulgences of the Orb of Thy grace which shineth from the horizon of Thy Name, the Ever-Forgiving, to grant me Thy pardon and to have mercy upon me. Write down, then, for me with Thy pen of glory that which will exalt me through Thy Name in the world of creation. Aid me, O my Lord, to set myself towards Thee, and to hearken unto the voice of Thy loved ones, whom the powers of the earth have failed to weaken, and the dominion of the nations has been powerless to withhold from Thee, and who, advancing towards Thee, have said: "God is our Lord, the Lord of all who are in heaven and all who are on earth." — Bahá'u'lláh [91]

The Station of Man

"We school you with the rule of wisdom and law, like unto a father who educateth his son, and this for naught but the protection of your own selves and the elevation of your stations." — Bahá'u'lláh [92]

Praise and Thanksgiving

"Thank God I see you spiritual and at rest; I give you this message from God; that you must be turned toward Him. Praise God that you are near Him! The unworthy things of this world have not deterred you from seeking the world of Spirit. When in harmony with that world, you care not for the things that perish; your desire is for that which never dies and the Kingdom lies open before you. I hope that the teaching of God will spread throughout the world, and will cause all to be united."

— 'Abdu'l-Bahá [93]

– Notes –

Reflection: If my vain imagination keeps me from fully recognizing Bahá'u'lláh and the fullness of His Revelation, here is a list of things I can do to make healthy shifts in my life right now. Do I watch too much TV? Am I distracted by material things? Am I attracted toward that which is unworthy on the internet? Do I participate in Feast regularly? Do I create/host a devotional program or volunteer in my local Bahá'í community? I could also monitor and write down my vain imaginings and idle fancies just to see them in black and white.

Reflection: As I consider my faithfulness to the Cause of Bahá'u'lláh and his Teachings, let me recall His Faithfulness to God in carrying out His Mission. What are some key ways Bahá'u'lláh showed His faithfulness? How does His sacrifice compare to what I would need to do to set out on a path of Faithfulness to Him?

Meditation 10

Freedom, Responsibility and Chastity

Idle Fancies and Vain Imaginings

"Lauded be Thy name, O my God! I entreat Thee by the fragrances of the Raiment of Thy grace which at Thy bidding and in conformity with Thy desire were diffused throughout the entire creation, and by the Day-Star of Thy will that hath shone brightly, through the power of Thy might and of Thy sovereignty, above the horizon of Thy mercy, to blot out from my heart all idle fancies and vain imaginings, that with all my affections I may turn unto Thee, O Thou Lord of all mankind!

"I am Thy servant and the son of Thy servant, O my God! I have laid hold on the handle of Thy grace, and clung to the cord of Thy tender mercy. Ordain for me the good things that are with Thee, and nourish me from the Table Thou didst send down out of the clouds of Thy bounty and the heaven of Thy favor.

"Thou, in very truth, art the Lord of the worlds, and the God of all that are in heaven and all that are on earth."
— Bahá'u'lláh [94]

Faithfulness and Chastity

"The question you raise as to the place in one's life that a deep bond of love with someone we meet other than our husband or wife can have is easily defined in view of the teachings. Chastity implies both before and after marriage an unsullied, chaste sex life. Before marriage absolutely chaste, after marriage absolutely faithful to one's chosen companion. Faithful in all sexual acts, faithful in word and in deed." — Shoghi Effendi [95]

The Fear of God

"Every cause needeth a helper. In this Revelation the hosts which can render it victorious are the hosts of praiseworthy deeds and upright character. The leader and commander of these hosts hath ever been the fear of God, a fear that encompasseth all things, and reigneth over all things." — Bahá'u'lláh [96]

Strict Observance of the Divine Will

"The beginning of all things is the knowledge of God, and the end of all things is strict observance of whatsoever hath been sent down from the empyrean of the Divine Will that pervadeth all that is in the heavens and all that is on the earth." — Bahá'u'lláh [97]

"O SON OF SPIRIT! There is no peace for thee save by renouncing thyself and turning unto Me...."
— Bahá'u'lláh [98]

Forgiveness and Mercy

"Say: The sincere soul longeth for nearness to God even as the suckling babe yearneth for its mother's breast, nay more ardent is his longing, could ye but know it! Again, his longing is even as the panting of one sore athirst after the living waters of grace, or the yearning of the sinner for forgiveness and mercy. Thus do We expound unto you the mysteries of the Cause, and impart unto you what shall render you independent of all that hath so far occupied you, that perchance ye may enter the Court of Holiness within this exalted Paradise."
— Bahá'u'lláh [99]

Prayer for Forgiveness

"Glorified art Thou, O Lord my God! Every time I venture to make mention of Thee, I am held back by my mighty sins and grievous trespasses against Thee, and find myself wholly deprived of The grace, and utterly powerless to celebrate Thy praise. My great confidence in Thy bounty, however, reviveth my hope in Thee, and my certitude that Thou wilt bountifully deal with me emboldeneth me to extol Thee, and ask of Thee the things Thou dost possess.

"I implore Thee, O my God, by Thy mercy that hath surpassed all created things, and to which all that are immersed beneath the oceans of Thy names bear witness, not to abandon me unto myself, for my heart is prone to evil. Guard me, then, within the stronghold of Thy protection and the shelter of Thy care."

— Bahá'u'lláh [100]

The Station of Man

"Hold fast to the fear of God and firmly adhere to what is right. Verily I say, the tongue is for mentioning what is good, defile it not with unseemly talk. God hath forgiven what is past. Henceforward everyone should utter that which is meet and seemly, and should refrain from slander, abuse and whatever causeth sadness in men. Lofty is the station of man! Not long ago this exalted Word streamed forth from the treasury of Our Pen of Glory: Great and blessed is this Day – the Day in which all that lay latent in man hath been and will be made manifest. Lofty is the station of man, were he to hold fast to righteousness and truth and to remain firm and steadfast in the Cause. In the eyes of the All-Merciful a true man appeareth even as a firmament; its sun and moon are his sight and hearing, and his shining and resplendent character its stars. His is the loftiest station, and his influence educateth the world of being."

— Bahá'u'lláh [101]

Faithful

Praise God

"Praise be to Thee, O Lord, my Best Beloved! Make me steadfast in Thy Cause, and grant that I may be reckoned among those who have not violated Thy Covenant nor followed the gods of their own idle fancy."

— The Báb [102]

Reflection: When I turn unto God with all my affections and hold firmly to his grace and mercy, He will nourish me from His heaven (the Word of God). I am helpless if I do not turn toward him. I have had familial guidance that taught me to value religion but there is also a larger community that has drawn me into an understanding of a spiritual life. For that I am grateful, because many are wandering, bereft of relationships that provide spiritual accompaniment for their journey. May we seek out the righteous and remain grateful for God's guidance.

Reflection: I know the difference between deep bonds of love with friends within and outside of the Faith and tempting attractions that have paralized me with fantasy. And difficult experiences of my life have taught me that the path to an upright character is the fear of God. Am I faithful in all sexual acts, "faithful in word and in deed?"

Reflection: The path to an upright character is dependent upon adopting the Law of God and walking to the best of my ability, the path that will educate me in a spiritual as well as a physical world. The goal is to balance freedom and liberty with responsibility and obedience. In this individualistic society I have a great deal of freedom and liberty, which means I must be even more diligent in practicing responsibility and obedience.

Meditation 11

Connecting My Heart to Bahá'u'lláh

Idle Fancies and Vain Imaginings

"Thou beholdest, O my God, how every bone in my body soundeth like a pipe with the music of Thine inspiration, revealing the signs of Thy oneness and the clear tokens of Thy unity. I entreat Thee, O my God, by Thy Name which irradiateth all things, to raise up such servants as shall incline their ears to the voice of the melodies that hath ascended from the right hand of the throne of Thy glory. Make them, then, to quaff from the hand of Thy grace the wine of Thy mercy, that it may assure their hearts, and cause them to turn away from the left hand of idle fancies and vain imaginings to the right hand of confidence and certitude.

"Now that Thou hast guided them unto the door of Thy grace, O my Lord, cast them not away, by Thy bounty; and now that Thou hast summoned them unto the horizon of Thy Cause, keep them not back from Thee, by Thy graciousness and favor. Powerful art Thou to do as Thou pleasest. No God is there but Thee, the Omniscient, the All-Informed." — Bahá'u'lláh [104]

The Fear of God

"The first word which the Abha Pen hath revealed and inscribed on the first leaf of Paradise is this: "Verily I say: The fear of God hath ever been a sure defence and a safe stronghold for all the peoples of the world. It is the chief cause of the protection of mankind, and the supreme instrument for its preservation. Indeed, there existeth in man a faculty which deterreth him from, and guardeth him against, whatever is unworthy and unseemly, and which is known as his sense of shame. This, however, is confined to but a few; all have not possessed, and do not possess, it. It is incumbent upon the kings and the spiritual leaders of the world to lay fast hold on religion, inasmuch as through it the fear of God is instilled in all else but Him." — Baha'u'llah[105]

Chastity and Nobler People

"What Bahá'u'lláh means by chastity certainly does not include the kissing that goes on in modern society. It is detrimental to the morals of young people, and often leads them to go too far, or arouses appetites which they cannot perhaps at the time satisfy legitimately through marriage, and the suppression of which is a strain on them.

"The Bahá'í standard is very high, more particularly when compared with the thoroughly rotten morals of the present world. But this standard of ours will produce healthier, happier, nobler people, and induce stabler marriages." — Shoghi Effendi[106]

Prayer for Forgiveness and Mercy

"O God, my God! Have mercy then upon my helpless state, my poverty, my misery, my abasement! Give me to drink from the generous cup of Thy grace and forgiveness, stir me with the sweet scents of Thy love, gladden my bosom with the light of Thy knowledge, purify my soul with the mysteries of Thy oneness, raise me to life with the gentle breeze that cometh from the gardens of Thy mercy – till I sever myself from all else but Thee, and lay hold of the hem of Thy garment of grandeur, and consign to oblivion all that is not Thee, and be companioned by the sweet breathings that waft during these Thy days, and attain unto faithfulness at Thy Threshold of Holiness, and arise to serve Thy Cause, and to be humble before Thy loved ones, and, in the presence of Thy favoured ones, to be nothingness itself." — 'Abdu'l-Bahá [107]

Nobility of Man

"From the exalted source, and out of the essence of His favor and bounty He hath entrusted every created thing with a sign of His knowledge, so that none of His creatures may be deprived of its share in expressing, each according to its capacity and rank, this knowledge. This sign is the mirror of His beauty in the world of creation. The greater the effort exerted for the refinement of this sublime and noble mirror, the more faithfully will it be made to reflect the glory of the names and attributes of God, and reveal the wonders of His signs and knowledge. Every created thing will be enabled (so great is this reflecting power) to reveal the potentialities of its pre-ordained station, will recognize its capacity and limitations, and will testify to the truth that 'He, verily, is God; there is none other God besides Him.'...

"There can be no doubt whatever that, in consequence of the efforts which every man may consciously exert and as a result of the exertion of his own spiritual faculties, this mirror can be so cleansed from the dross of earthly defilements and purged from satanic fancies as to be able to draw nigh unto the meads of eternal holiness and attain the courts of everlasting tranquility."

— Bahá'u'lláh [108]

Praise God

"O thou possessor of a seeing heart! Although, materially speaking, thou art deprived of physical sight, yet, praise be to God, spiritual insight is thine. Thy heart seeth and thy spirit heareth. Bodily sight is subject to a thousand maladies and assuredly will ultimately be lost. Thus no importance should be attached to it. But the sight of the heart is illumined. It discerneth and discovereth the divine Kingdom. It is everlasting and eternal. Praise God, therefore, that the sight of thy heart is illumined, and the hearing of thy mind responsive." — 'Abdu'l-Bahá [109]

Faithful

Reflection: This selection of Writings brings assurance to my heart that if I forego idle fancies and vain imaginings, His mercy will cause me to feel confidence and certitude. Can I give Him less than my whole heart when He summons me with His Revelation? Do I see the pattern? Repentance of vain imaginings fortified by assurance of my heart? Can I also see the place that self-forgiveness plays in this pattern? Once I take responsibility for my behavior, God gives me assurance, attracts me through his mercifulness; and I can then forgive myself in repentance.

Reflection: Until today I have never connected the "fear of God" with "Paradise." Bahá'u'lláh says all do not possess shame. What are the indications that I possess the fear of God? How do I guard myself against those who do not possess it? I know I possess shame; but since I have been created noble, I will accept Bahá'u'lláh's protection and believe Him when He says there is a connection between the fear of God and Paradise.

Reflection: In the Kitab-i-Aqdas, Bahá'u'lláh has set limits and boundaries for me and calls me to a higher standard. I am in a state of misery if I do not know how to set boundaries for others who might intrude upon my marriage. Conversely, I can cause a lot of misery to others if I do not honor their boundaries. What experiences or lessons have I had that have shown me the need for boundaries?

Meditation 12

Verily Thy Lovers Thirst for Chastity!

Idle Fancies and Vain Imaginings
"I implore Thee, O Thou Fashioner of the nations and the King of eternity, to guard Thy handmaidens within the tabernacle of Thy chastity, and to cancel such of their deeds as are unworthy of Thy days. Purge out, then, from them, O my God, all doubts and idle fancies, and sanctify them from whatsoever becometh not their kinship with Thee, O Thou Who art the Lord of names, and the Source of utterance. Thou art He in Whose grasp are the reins of the entire creation.

"No God is there but Thee, the Almighty, the Most Exalted, the All-Glorious, the Self-Subsisting."

— Bahá'u'lláh [110]

Spotless Chastity
"There is no need to dwell at length on the implications of spotless chastity and the integrity of the sacred marital bond set forth in our teachings, as these have been clearly outlined and amply elaborated in our scriptures and in the writings of our beloved Guardian. Such matters as the age of marriage or the manner of meeting economic commitments are left to the individual to decide for himself. The friends, however, should not hesitate to seek the advice of their local Spiritual Assemblies in all such matters if they feel the need. "As the suffering and unrest afflicting humanity increase, and moral restraints are one by one abolished, the Bahá'ís must learn to obtain, through study and prayer, a clearer vision of their mission, earnestly seek to purge their lives of the influences of laity and promiscuity characterizing

Faithful

modern society, and insure that the fair name and integrity of the Faith they serve and love so dearly remain unstained and unsullied."

— Universal House of Justice[111]

Forgiveness

"O army of God! Beware lest ye harm any soul, or make any heart to sorrow; lest ye wound any man with your words, be he known to you or a stranger, be he friend or foe. Pray ye for all; ask ye that all be blessed, all be forgiven. Beware, beware, lest any of you seek vengeance, even against one who is thirsting for your blood. Beware, beware, lest ye offend the feelings of another, even though he be an evil-doer, and he wish you ill. Look ye not upon the creatures, turn ye to their Creator. See ye not the never-yielding people, see but the Lord of Hosts. Gaze ye not down upon the dust, gaze upward at the shining sun, which hath caused every patch of darksome earth to glow with light."

—'Abdu'l-Baha[112]

Prayer for Forgiveness and Grace

"Thou seest me, O my God, bowed down in lowliness, humbling myself before Thy commandments, submitting to Thy sovereignty, trembling at the might of Thy dominion, fleeing from Thy wrath, entreating Thy grace, relying upon Thy forgiveness, shaking with awe at Thy fury. I implore Thee with a throbbing heart, with streaming tears and a yearning soul, and in complete detachment from all things, to make Thy lovers as rays of light across Thy realms, and to aid Thy chosen servants to exalt Thy Word, that their faces may turn beauteous and bright with splendour, that their hearts may be filled with mysteries, and that every soul may lay down its burden of sin. Guard them then from the aggressor, from him who hath become a shameless and blasphemous doer of wrong.

"Verily Thy lovers thirst, O my Lord; lead them to the wellspring of bounty and grace. Verily, they hunger; send down unto them Thy heavenly table. Verily, they are naked; robe them in the garments of learning and knowledge. Verily Thou art He of abounding grace. There is none other God save Thee, the Mighty, the Powerful, the Ever-Bestowing."
— 'Abdu'l-Baha[113]

Nobility of Man

"O SON OF SPIRIT!
I created thee rich, why dost thou bring thyself down to poverty? Noble I made thee, wherewith dost thou abase thyself? Out of the essence of knowledge I gave thee being, why seekest thou enlightenment from anyone beside Me? Out of the clay of love I molded thee, how dost thou busy thyself with another? Turn thy sight unto thyself, that thou mayest find Me standing within thee, mighty, powerful and self-subsisting."
— Baha'u'llah[114]

Praise God

"We yield praise unto God – hallowed and glorified be He – for whatsoever He hath graciously revealed in this blessed, this glorious and incomparable Day. Indeed if everyone on earth were endowed with a myriad tongues and were to continually praise God and magnify His Name to the end that knoweth no end, their thanksgiving would not prove adequate for even one of the gracious favours We have mentioned in this Tablet. Unto this beareth witness every man of wisdom and discernment, of understanding and knowledge."
— Baha'u'llah[115]

Reflection: The purging of all doubts and fancies is not something that happens once in our lifetime. It's an ongoing process that we obtain through daily study of the Writings and prayer. Victory comes as the veils of modern society are lifted and we see clearly. I am determined to lay the foundation of love within my marriage; I am determined to recognize the idle fancies that separate me from God and a true relationship with my spouse (whether I am a man or a woman) because I thirst for Chastity!

Reflection: Though I may not be able to keep someone in my life who is violating my boundaries, 'Abdu'l-Bahá indicates that I should pray for them to receive blessings and forgiveness. I also need to recognize my participation in the violation of my boundaries. What nugget of truth have I learned from those who have violated my boundaries? And what nugget of truth have I received from my own lessons of chastity?

Meditation 13

Detachment from Divergent Views of Sexual Behavior in the World

Idle Fancies and Vain Imaginings

"I beg of Thee, O my God, by Thy power, and Thy might, and Thy sovereignty, which have embraced all who are in Thy heaven and on Thy earth, to make known unto Thy servants this luminous Way and this straight Path, that they may acknowledge Thy unity and Thy oneness, with a certainty which the vain imaginations of the doubters will not impair, nor the idle fancies of the wayward obscure. Illumine, O my Lord, the eyes of Thy servants, and brighten their hearts with the splendors of the light of Thy knowledge, that they may apprehend the greatness of this most sublime station, and recognize this most luminous Horizon, that haply the clamor of men may fail to deter them from turning their gaze towards the effulgent light of Thy unity, and to hinder them from setting their faces toward the Horizon of detachment."

— Baha'u'llah[116]

Chastity and Marriage

"With reference to the question you have asked concerning the Bahá'í attitude towards the problem of sex and its relation to marriage.

"The Bahá'í Teachings on this matter, which is of such vital concern and about which there is a wide divergency of views, are very clear and emphatic. Briefly stated the Bahá'í conception of sex is based on the belief that chastity should be strictly practiced by both sexes, not only because it is in itself highly commendable ethically, but

also due to its being the only way to a happy and successful marital life. Sex relationships of any form, outside marriage, are not permissible..."
— Shoghi Effendi[117]

"Think not that we have revealed unto you a mere code of laws. Nay, rather, We have unsealed the choice Wine with the fingers of might and power. To this beareth witness that which the Pen of Revelation hath revealed. Meditate on this, O men of insight" — Baha'u'llah[118]

"Purity and chastity...have been, and still are, the most great ornaments for the handmaidens of God. God is my witness! The brightness of the light of chastity sheddeth it's illumination upon the worlds of the spirit, and its fragrance is wafted even unto the Most Exalted Paradise." — Baha'u'llah[119]

"Bahá'í marriage is the commitment of two parties one to the other and their mutual attachment of mind and heart. Each must, however, exercise the utmost care to become thoroughly acquainted with the character of the other, that the binding covenant between them may be a tie that will endure forever. Their purpose must be this: to become loving companions and comrades and at one with each other for time and eternity.....

The true marriage of Bahá'ís is this, that husband and wife should be united both physically and spiritually, that they may ever improve the spiritual life of each other, and may enjoy everlasting unity throughout all the worlds of God. This is Bahá'í marriage." — 'Abdu'l-Baha[120]

Prayer for Forgiveness

"O Thou forgiving Lord! Thou art the shelter of all these Thy servants. Thou knowest the secrets and art aware of all things. We are all helpless, and Thou art the Mighty, the Omnipotent. We are all sinners, and Thou art the Forgiver of sins, the Merciful, the Compassionate. O Lord! Look not at our shortcomings. Deal with us according to Thy grace and bounty. Our shortcomings are many, but the ocean of Thy forgiveness is boundless. Our weakness is grievous, but the evidences of Thine aid and assistance are clear. Therefore, confirm and strengthen us. Enable us to do that which is worthy of Thy holy Threshold. Illumine our hearts, grant us discerning eyes and attentive ears. Resuscitate the dead and heal the sick. Bestow wealth upon the poor and give peace and security to the fearful. Accept us in Thy kingdom and illumine us with the light of guidance. Thou art the Powerful and the Omnipotent. Thou art the Generous. Thou art the Clement. Thou art the Kind."

— 'Abdu'l-Baha[121]

Nobility of Man

"O SON OF SPIRIT!

"Noble have I created thee, yet thou hast abased thyself. Rise then unto that for which thou wast created"

— Baha'u'llah.[122]

— *Notes* —

Spotless Chastity:
"There is no doubt that the standard of spotless chastity inculcated by Bahá'u'lláh in His teachings can be attained by the friends only when they stand forth firmly and courageously as uncompromising adherents of the Bahá'í way of life, fully conscious that they represent teachings which are the very antithesis of the corrosive forces which are so tragically destroying the fabric of man's moral values. The present trend in modern society with our challenging principles of moral conduct, far from influencing the believers to compromise their resolve to adhere undeviatingly to the standards of purity and chastity, set forth for them by their faith, must stimulate them to discharge their sacred obligations with determination and thus combat the evil forces undermining the foundations of individual morality."

— Universal House of Justice[123]

— *Notes* —

Reflection: A friend of mine once explained "detachment" to be detachment from the world and attachment to God or the Writings. God has not left me alone in this world without guidance regarding sex and marriage. Looking back through history we can see God's hand working through millennia.[124] What verses in the Writings reassure me and give me certitude that chastity is the only way to a happy and successful marital life? What verses assure me that even though I am weak, if I pray for discerning eyes and attentive ears, God will confirm and strengthen me?

Reflection: I was a child who was trained by an authority figure to be immoral from a very young age. Perhaps you, too, were sexually abused as a child and experienced pleasure from it, as I did. Speaking the truth about this is not a confession. You did nothing wrong, but as an adult it is time to take responsibility for your behavior if you are addicted to sexuality and are having multiple partners. The more you talk about this, the more you will be validated that it was not your fault. There are groups you can turn to.[125] There may be someone in your Bahá'í Community you can turn to. Keep searching, keep praying, and keep believing that Bahá'u'lláh is seeking your good. When I first started attending a support group to talk about the abuse that happened to me, I found that I couldn't verbalize it. That facet of my identity was non-verbal. I spoke like a child and had to develop language for it. In the course of time, I was externally validated over and over again and no longer believe it was my fault.

Faithful

Notes

Meditation 14

Of Saints and Trusted Servants

Idle Fancies and Vain Imaginings

"I entreat Thee, therefore, O my God, by Thy Name through which Thou hast guided Thy lovers to the living waters of Thy grace and Thy favors, and attracted them that long for Thee to the Paradise of Thy nearness and Thy presence, to open the eyes of Thy people that they may recognize in this Revelation the manifestation of Thy transcendent unity, and the dawning of the lights of Thy countenance and Thy beauty. Cleanse them, then, O my God, from all idle fancies and vain imaginations, that they may inhale the fragrances of sanctity from the robe of Thy Revelation and Thy commandment, that haply they may cease to inflict upon me what will deprive their souls of the fragrances of the manifold tokens of Thy mercy, that are wafted in the days of Him Who is the Manifestation of Thyself, and the Day-Spring of Thy Cause, and that they may not perpetrate what will call down Thy wrath and anger." — Baha'u'llah[126]

Submissiveness and Chastity

"O Handmaids of the Self-Sustaining Lord! Exert your efforts so that you may attain the honour and privilege ordained for women. Undoubtedly the greatest glory of women is servitude at His Threshold and submissiveness at His door; it is the possession of a vigilant heart, and praise of the incomparable God; it is heartfelt love towards other handmaids and spotless chastity...."

'Abdu'l-Baha[127]

Faithful

Prayer for Forgiveness
"O Lord, Thou possessor of infinite mercy! O Lord of forgiveness and pardon! Forgive our sins, pardon our shortcomings, and cause us to turn to the kingdom of Thy clemency, invoking the kingdom of might and power, humble at Thy shrine and submissive before the glory of Thine evidences.

"O Lord God! Make us as waves of the sea, as flowers of the garden, united, agreed through the bounties of Thy love. O Lord! Dilate the breasts through the signs of Thy oneness, and make all mankind as stars shining from the same height of glory, as perfect fruits growing upon Thy tree of life.

"Verily, Thou art the Almighty, the Self-Subsistent, the Giver, the Forgiving, the Pardoner, the Omniscient, the One Creator." — 'Abdu'l-Baha[128]

Nobility of Man
"O saints of God! at the end of Our discourse We enjoin on you once again chastity, faithfulness, godliness, sincerity, and purity. Lay aside the evil and adopt the good. This is that whereunto ye are commanded in the Book of God, the Knowing, the Wise. Well is it with those who practice [this injunction]. At this moment the pen crieth out, saying, 'O saints of God, regard the horizon of uprightness, and be quit, severed, and free from what is beside this. There is no strength and no power save in God." — 'Abdu'l-Baha[129]

Praise God
"We yield praise unto God — hallowed and glorified be He — for whatsoever He hath graciously revealed in this blessed, this glorious and incomparable Day. Indeed if everyone on earth were endowed with a myriad tongues and were to continually praise God and mag-

nify His Name to the end that knoweth no end, their thanksgiving would not prove adequate for even one of the gracious favours We have mentioned in this Tablet. Unto this beareth witness every man of wisdom and discernment, of understanding and knowledge."

— Baha'u'llah[130]

Reflection: Bahá'u'lláh entreats God to cleanse us from "all idle fancies and vain imaginations" in the prayer in this chapter...He calls us to sanctity through His Revelation and commandments. And in yet another quotation 'Abdu'l-Bahá exhorts women to attain their highest glory, which is servitude at His Threshold. Given that there are so many prayers for forgiveness and for our helplessness, do you think it is impossible to maintain spotless chastity? What are the physical and mental results of endlessly shaming oneself instead of believing in God's forgiveness, our nobility, and maintaining a vigilant heart? What is "spotless chastity? And how can I achieve it?

Reflection: We cannot say: "I can never be perfect, so it's OK to make mistakes, I shouldn't feel bad when I do, because God forgives me." While perfection is by definition unattainable, that cannot be used an excuse for our shortcomings. Rather, we continually strive to draw closer to that ideal standard, both inwardly and outwardly, bearing in mind our imperfection but also our great potential and God's assistance. This is where the Bahá'í principle of calling ourselves to account at the end of the day is essential AND saying the name of Bahá'u'lláh at every moment we even think of going off the straight path will help us maintain spotless chastity. And if you are not a Bahá'í, you can certainly say the name of the Prophet that is meaningful to you. Thus you will have the fortitude to have both spotless behaviour and thoughts.

Faithful

Reflection: Bahá'u'lláh calls me to my noble station through immersing myself in His Book. Wouldn't it be incongruent if I did not arise to assist the Cause of God by teaching children's classes, holding devotionals, attending Feasts and cluster meetings? What confirmations have I received in the past by assisting the Cause of God?

Reflection: In the Traveller's Narrative, 'Abdu'l-Bahá is calling us "O Saints of God" and calling us to nobility through the virtues he has listed. Do you realize that you are a Saint and a Noble, trusted servant of God?

Meditation 15

A Saint in a State of Grievous Abasement?

Idle Fancies and Vain Imaginings
"Every man of insight will, in this day, readily admit that the counsels which the Pen of this Wronged One hath revealed constitute the supreme animating power for the advancement of the world and the exaltation of its peoples. Arise, O people, and, by the power of God's might, resolve to gain the victory over your own selves, that haply the whole earth may be freed and sanctified from its servitude to the gods of its idle fancies – gods that have inflicted such loss upon, and are responsible for the misery of their wretched worshippers. These idols form the obstacle that impedeth man in his efforts to advance in the path of perfection. We cherish the hope that the Hand of divine power may lend its assistance to mankind and deliver it from its state of grievous abasement."

— Baha'u'llah[131]

Wisdom
"The essence of wisdom is the fear of God, the dread of His scourge and punishment, and the apprehension of His justice and decree"

— Baha'u'llah.[132]

Prayer for Forgiveness and Pardon
"O Thou compassionate, almighty One! This assemblage of souls have turned their faces unto Thee in supplication. With the utmost humility and submission they look toward Thy Kingdom and beg Thee for pardon and forgiveness. O God! Endear this assembly to Thyself. Sanctify these souls, and cast upon them the rays of Thy

guidance. Illumine their hearts, and gladden their spirits with Thy glad tidings. Receive all of them in Thy holy Kingdom; confer upon them Thine inexhaustible bounty; make them happy in this world and in the world to come. O God! We are weak; give us strength. We are poor; bestow upon us Thine illimitable treasures. We are sick; grant unto us Thy divine healing. We are impotent; give us Thy heavenly power. O Lord! Make us useful in this world; free us from the condition of self and desire. O Lord! Make us brethren in Thy love, and cause us to be loving toward all Thy children. Confirm us in service to the world of humanity so that we may become the servants of Thy servants, that we may love all Thy creatures and become compassionate to all Thy people. O Lord, Thou art the Almighty. Thou art the Merciful. Thou art the Forgiver. Thou art the Omnipotent."

— Abdu'l-Baha[133]

Nobility of Man

"From the exalted source, and out of the essence of His favor and bounty He hath entrusted every created thing with a sign of His knowledge, so that none of His creatures may be deprived of its share in expressing, each according to its capacity and rank, this knowledge. This sign is the mirror of His beauty in the world of creation. The greater the effort exerted for the refinement of this sublime and noble mirror, the more faithfully will it be made to reflect the glory of the names and attributes of God, and reveal the wonders of His signs and knowledge. Every created thing will be enabled (so great is this reflecting power) to reveal the potentialities of its pre-ordained station, will recognize its capacity and limitations, and will testify to the truth that "He, verily, is God; there is none other God besides Him."...

There can be no doubt whatever that, in consequence of the efforts which every man may consciously exert and as a result of the exertion of his own spiritual faculties, this mirror can be so cleansed from the dross of earthly defilements and purged from satanic fancies as to be able to draw nigh unto the meads of eternal holiness and attain the courts of everlasting fellowship."
— *Baha'u'llah*[134]

Praise God

"The people of the world are the tools in His hand. They must strive to understand His message and to walk in the path of His divine guidance. Every human being is responsible in this day to seek the truth for himself and thereafter to live according to that wise counsel. The old ones have all longed for this sweet message. Praise God that you have found it."
— Universal House of Justice [135]

— Notes —

Reflection: When I serve the "gods" of my idle fancies, my deeds will not be virtuous. What virtues do I need to develop in order to remove the obstacles in my path toward perfection?

Reflection: God has bestowed upon me spiritual faculties that are destined to cleanse and purge my mirror of satanic fancies, enabling me to walk in the path of His divine guidance. What can I do each day to make sure I can be a tool of God? Am I striving to understand what His message means and how it applies to all the facets of my life, my marriage, my relationships, my place in my Bahá'í community?

Meditation 16

Let Each Morn Be Better than Its Eve

Idle Fancies and Vain Imaginings

"O peoples of the world! Forsake all evil, hold fast that which is good. Strive to be shining examples unto all mankind, and true reminders of the virtues of God amidst men. He that riseth to serve My Cause should manifest My wisdom, and bend every effort to banish ignorance from the earth. Be united in counsel, be one in thought. Let each morn be better than its eve and each morrow richer than its yesterday. Man's merit lieth in service and virtue and not in the pageantry of wealth and riches. Take heed that your words be purged from idle fancies and worldly desires and your deeds be cleansed from craftiness and suspicion. Dissipate not the wealth of your precious lives in the pursuit of evil and corrupt affection, nor let your endeavours be spent in promoting your personal interest. Be generous in your days of plenty, and be patient in the hour of loss. Adversity is followed by success and rejoicings follow woe. Guard against idleness and sloth, and cling unto that which profiteth mankind, whether young or old, whether high or low. Beware lest ye sow tares of dissension among men or plant thorns of doubt in pure and radiant hearts."
— Baha'u'llah[136]

Faithfulness and Chastity

"O friends of God, verily the Pen of Sincerity enjoineth on you the greatest faithfulness. By the Life of God, its light is more evident than the light of the sun! In its light and its brightness and its radiance every light is eclipsed. We desire of God that He will not withhold from His

cities and lands the radiant effulgence of the Sun of Faithfulness. We have directed all in the nights and in the days to faithfulness, chastity, purity, and constancy; and have enjoined good deeds and well-pleasing qualities."
— 'Abdu'l-Baha[137]

Prayer for Forgiveness

"Beware that ye deny not the favor of God after it hath been sent down unto you. Better is this for you than that which ye possess; for that which is yours perisheth, whilst that which is with God endureth. He, in truth, ordaineth what He pleaseth. Verily, the breezes of forgiveness have been wafted from the direction of your Lord, the God of Mercy; whoso turneth thereunto, shall be cleansed of his sins, and of all pain and sickness. Happy the man that hath turned towards them, and woe betide him that hath turned aside." — Baha'u'llah[138]

Nobility of Man

"Also in the tradition of Kumayl[139] it is written: 'Behold, a light hath shone forth out of the morn of eternity, and lo, its waves have penetrated the inmost reality of all men.' Man, the noblest and most perfect of all created things, excelleth them all in the intensity of this revelation, and is a fuller expression of its glory."
— Baha'u'llah[140]

Praise Be to God

O NOBLE friends; seekers after God! Praise be to God! Today the light of Truth is shining upon the world in its abundance; the breezes of the heavenly garden are blowing throughout all regions; the call of the Kingdom is heard in all lands, and the breath of the Holy Spirit is felt in all hearts that are faithful. The Spirit of God is giving eternal life. In this wonderful age the East is enlightened, the West is fragrant, and everywhere the soul inhales the holy perfume. The sea of the unity of mankind is lifting up its waves with joy, for there is real communication between the hearts and minds of men. The banner of the Holy Spirit is uplifted, and men see it, and are assured with the knowledge that this is a new day.

This is a new cycle of human power. All the horizons of the world are luminous, and the world will become indeed as a garden and a paradise. It is the hour of unity of the sons of men and of the drawing together of all races and all classes. You are loosed from ancient superstitions which have kept men ignorant, destroying the foundation of true humanity.

The gift of God to this enlightened age is the knowledge of the oneness of mankind and of the fundamental oneness of religion. War shall cease between nations, and by the will of God the Most Great Peace shall come; the world will be seen as a new world, and all men will live as brothers." — 'Abdu'l-Baha[141]

– Notes –

Reflection: Living an unchaste life means my deeds and thoughts will reflect my idle fancies. It is knowledge and wisdom that will cleanse my deeds from craftiness and suspicion. I will scan my history to remember times when I was degraded by ignorance, lack of faith, untruth and selfishness. How have I grown from the times that I have dissipated my efforts to serve the Cause of God because of passion? What can help me to "return" to God in repentance?

Reflection: My constant prayer is that each morning may be better than the night before. All I need to do is concentrate on one day at a time. "Abdu'l-Bahá says this is the hour of unity of the sons of men and a new cycle of human power. I will reach out to tap into the blessings and bounties of this new day that I am living in. The Writings are permeated with the message of unity. How can it not be true?

– Notes –

Meditation 17

If I Add up My Accomplishments Each Day, I Will Feel the Confirmations of God Supporting Me

Idle Fancies and Vain Imaginings

"The Heaven of true understanding shineth resplendent with the light of two luminaries: tolerance and righteousness. O my friend! Vast oceans lie enshrined within this brief saying. Blessed are they who appreciate its value, drink deep therefrom and grasp its meaning, and woe betide the heedless. This lowly one entreateth the people of the world to observe fairness, that their tender, their delicate and precious hearing which hath been created to hearken unto the words of wisdom may be freed from impediments and from such allusions, idle fancies or vain imaginings as 'cannot fatten nor appease the hunger', so that the true Counsellor may be graciously inclined to set forth that which is the source of blessing for mankind and of the highest good for all nations." — Baha'u'llah[142]

Forgiveness and Grace of God

"Say: O people! Withhold not from yourselves the grace of God and His mercy. Whoso withholdeth himself therefrom is indeed in grievous loss. What, O people! Do ye worship the dust, and turn away from your Lord, the Gracious, the All-Bountiful? Fear ye God, and be not of those who perish. Say: The Book of God hath been sent down in the form of this Youth. Hallowed, therefore, be God, the most excellent of makers! Take ye good heed, O peoples of the world, lest ye flee from His face. Nay, make haste to attain His presence, and be of them that have returned unto Him. Pray to be forgiven, O people, *for having failed in your duty towards God, and for having trespassed against His Cause, and be not of the foolish. He it is Who hath created you; He it is Who hath nourished your souls through His Cause, and enabled you to recognize Him Who is the Almighty, the Most Exalted, the All-Knowing. He it is Who hath unveiled to your eyes the treasures of His knowledge, and caused you to ascend unto the heaven of certitude – the certitude of His resistless, His irrefutable, and most exalted Faith. Beware that ye do not deprive yourselves of the grace of God, that ye do not bring to naught your works, and do not repudiate the truth of this most manifest, this lofty, this shining, and glorious Revelation. Judge ye fairly the Cause of God, your Creator, and behold that which hath been sent down from the Throne on high, and meditate thereon with innocent and sanctified hearts. Then will the truth of this Cause appear unto you as manifest as the sun in its noon-tide glory. Then will ye be of them that have believed in Him."*

— Baha'u'llah[143]

Chastity of Soul and Freedom of Spirit

"The understanding of His words and the comprehension of the utterances of the Birds of Heaven are in no wise dependent upon human learning. They depend solely upon purity of heart, chastity of soul, and freedom of spirit. This is evidenced by those who, today, though without a single letter of the accepted standards of learning, are occupying the loftiest seats of knowledge; and the garden of their hearts is adorned, through the showers of divine grace, with the roses of wisdom and the tulips of understanding. Well is it with the sincere in heart for their share of the light of a mighty Day!"

— Baha'u'llah[144]

Add up your accomplishments
"We must be patient with others, infinitely patient!, but also with our own poor selves, remembering that even the Prophets of God sometimes got tired and cried out in despair!...He urges you to persevere and add up your accomplishments, rather than to dwell on the dark side of things. Everyone's life has both a dark and bright side. The Master said: turn your back to the darkness and your face to me." — Shoghi Effendi[145]

Prayer for Forgiveness
"O God our Lord! Protect us through Thy grace from whatsoever may be repugnant unto Thee, and vouchsafe unto us that which well beseemeth Thee. Give us more out of Thy bounty, and bless us. Pardon us for the things we have done, and wash away our sins, and forgive us with Thy gracious forgiveness. Verily, Thou art the Most Exalted, the Self-Subsisting." — The Bab[146]

Nobility of Man
"Aim high, choose noble ends; how long this lethargy, how long this negligence! Despair, both here and hereafter, is all you will gain from self-indulgence; abomination and misery are all you will harvest from fanaticism, from believing the foolish and the mindless. The confirmations of God are supporting you, the succor of God is at hand: why do you not cry out and exult with all your heart, and strive with all your soul!" — 'Abdu'l-Baha[147]

Praise Be to God
"Praise be to God! the springtime of God is at hand. This century is verily the spring season. The world of mind and the kingdom of soul have become fresh and verdant by its bestowals. It has resuscitated the whole realm of existence. On one hand the lights of reality are shining; on the other the clouds of divine mercy are pouring down the fullness of heavenly bounty. Wonderful

Faithful

material progress is evident and great spiritual discoveries are being made. Truly this can be called the miracle of centuries for it is replete with manifestations of the miraculous. The time has come when all mankind shall be united, when all races shall be loyal to one fatherland, all religions become one religion and racial and religious bias pass away. It is a day in which the oneness of humankind shall uplift its standard and international peace like the true morning flood the world with its light. Therefore we offer supplications to God, asking him to dispel these gloomy clouds and uproot these imitations in order that the East and West may become radiant with love and unity; that the nations of the world shall embrace each other and the ideal spiritual brotherhood illumine the world like the glorious sun of the high heavens." — 'Abdu'l-Baha[148]

— Notes —

Reflection: Bahá'u'lláh wants justice for me...for you. In His Words of Wisdom He says, "*The essence of all that We have revealed for thee is Justice, is for man to free himself from idle fancy and imitation, discern with the eye of oneness His glorious handiwork, and look into all things with a searching eye.*" Baha'u'llah[149] In the verse above this one, He connects my sense of hearing to wisdom. He wants me to hear with my heart! How would my life change if I sought Justice within my marriage and detachment from someone who might destroy my marriage as a fortress of well-being, whether through my attraction or theirs? I want to rid myself of my idle fancies and vain imaginings and understand what constitutes true relationships. What are they like when not marred by false expectations?

Reflection: Many of us walk through life believing we are unworthy, but 'Abdu'l-Bahá says it is the recognition of Bahá'u'lláh that makes us worthy.[150] Bahá'u'lláh further proclaims that true knowledge depends upon "*purity of heart, chastity of soul and freedom of spirit.*" Repentance saves me from remoteness from God. What could I change in my life and marriage to make me feel worthy? Remember, bounty is not dependent on the best behavior. Bounty is freely given out of the love of God! So I must stop self-punishment! When I bring myself to account each day as Bahá'u'lláh tells me to do in the Hidden Words, I can also count the many wonderful things I have done as I add up my accomplishments!

– *Notes* –

Meditation 18

Strong Language from a Father Figure

Idle Fancies and Vain Imaginings

"O ye that dwell on earth! The religion of God is for love and unity; make it not the cause of enmity or dissension. In the eyes of men of insight and the beholders of the Most Sublime Vision, whatsoever are the effective means for safeguarding and promoting the happiness and welfare of the children of men have already been revealed by the Pen of Glory. But the foolish ones of the earth, being nurtured in evil passions and desires, have remained heedless of the consummate wisdom of Him Who is, in truth, the All-Wise, while their words and deeds are prompted by idle fancies and vain imaginings."

— Baha'u'llah[151]

Chastity and Fidelity

"Apart from these provisions Bahá'u'lláh exhorts His followers to consort, with amity and concord and without discrimination, with the adherents of all religions; warns them to guard against fanaticism, sedition, pride, dispute and contention; inculcates upon them immaculate cleanliness, strict truthfulness, spotless chastity, trustworthiness, hospitality, fidelity, courtesy, forbearance, justice and fairness; counsels them to be "even as the fingers of one hand and the limbs of one body"; calls upon them to arise and serve His Cause; and assures them of His undoubted aid."   — Shoghi Effendi[152]

Faithful

Returning to God and Repentance

"Thus have We recounted unto you the tales of the one true God, and sent down unto you the things He had preordained, that haply ye may ask forgiveness of Him, may return unto Him, may truly repent, may realize your misdeeds, may shake off your slumber, may be roused from your heedlessness, may atone for the things that have escaped you, and be of them that do good. Let him who will, acknowledge the truth of My words; and as to him that willeth not, let him turn aside. My sole duty is to remind you of your failure in duty towards the Cause of God, if perchance ye may be of them that heed My warning. Wherefore, hearken ye unto My speech, and return ye to God and repent, that He, through His grace, may have mercy upon you, may wash away your sins, and forgive your trespasses. The greatness of His mercy surpasseth the fury of His wrath, and His grace encompasseth all who have been called into being and been clothed with the robe of life, be they of the past or of the future." — Baha'u'llah[153]

Prayer for Forgiveness

"O God my God! Thou seest me standing before the door of Thy forgiveness and benevolence, turning my gaze toward the horizon of Thy bountiful favours and manifold blessings. I beg of Thee by Thy sweet accents and by the shrill voice of Thy Pen, O Lord of all mankind, to graciously aid Thy servants as it befitteth Thy days and beseemeth the glory of Thy manifestation and Thy majesty. Verily potent art Thou to do whatsoever Thou willest. All they that dwell in the heavens and on the earth bear witness to Thy power and Thy might, to Thy glory and Thy bounteousness. Praise be to Thee, O Lord of the worlds and the Well-Beloved of the heart of every man of understanding!

"Thou beholdest, O my God, the essence of poverty seeking the ocean of Thy wealth and the substance of iniquity yearning for the waters of Thy forgiveness and Thy tender mercy. Grant Thou, O my God, that which beseemeth Thy great glory and befitteth the loftiness of Thy boundless grace. Thou art in truth the All-Bountiful, the Lord of grace abounding, the Ordainer, the All-Wise. No God is there but Thee, the Most Powerful, the All-Compelling, the Omnipotent." — Baha'u'llah[154]

Nobility of Man

"Again, is there any deed in the world that would be nobler than service to the common good? Is there any greater blessing conceivable for a man, than that he should become the cause of the education, the development, the prosperity and honor of his fellow-creatures? No, by the Lord God! The highest righteousness of all is for blessed souls to take hold of the hands of the helpless and deliver them out of their ignorance and abasement and poverty, and with pure motives, and only for the sake of God, to arise and energetically devote themselves to the service of the masses, forgetting their own worldly advantage and working only to serve the general good. "They prefer them before themselves, though poverty be their own lot."[1] "The best of men are those who serve the people; the worst of men are those who harm the people." — 'Abdu'l-Baha[155]

[1 Qur'án 59:9.]

Praise Be to God

"*The powers of earth cannot withstand the privileges and bestowals which God has ordained for this great and glorious century. It is a need and exigency of the time. Man can withstand anything except that which is divinely intended and indicated for the age and its requirements. Now, Praise be to God! in all countries of the world, lovers of peace are to be found and these principles are being spread among mankind, especially in this country. Praise be to God! this thought is prevailing and souls are continually arising as defenders of the oneness of humanity, endeavoring to assist and establish international peace. There is no doubt that this wonderful democracy will be able to realize it and the banner of international agreement will be unfurled here to spread onward and outward among all the nations of the world. I give thanks to God that I find you imbued with such susceptibilities and lofty aspirations and I hope that you will be the means of spreading this light to all men. Thus may the Sun of Reality shine upon the East and West. The enveloping clouds shall pass away and the heat of the divine rays will dispel the mist. The reality of man shall develop and come forth as the image of God his creator. The thoughts of man shall take such upward flight that former accomplishments shall appear as the play of children; — for the ideas and beliefs of the past and the prejudices regarding race and religion have ever been lowering and destructive to human evolution. I am most hopeful that in this century these lofty thoughts shall be conducive to human welfare. Let this century be the sun of previous centuries the effulgences of which shall last forever, so that in times to come they shall glorify the twentieth century, saying the twentieth century was the century of lights, the twentieth century was the century of life, the twentieth century was the century of international peace, the twentieth century was the century of divine bestowals and the twentieth century has left traces which shall last forever."* — *'Abdu'l-Baha*[156]

Reflection: I am dumbfounded that I am privileged to live in this century. I don't want time to slip away from me! How could I disappoint 'Abdu'l-Bahá's hope that I will be the means of spreading this light to all men and that my thoughts would remain lofty, taking an upward flight privately and publicly? If I allow Bahá'u'lláh's Revelation to regenerate me through the Holy Spirit, I will be doing my part to assist Bahá'u'lláh in regenerating the world.

Reflection: Bahá'u'lláh is offering me the knowledge of God with the Pen of Glory! How can that compare with words and deeds that are "prompted by idle fancies and vain imaginings?" Do I believe it when Bahá'u'lláh assures me of His undoubted aid? What would make me a believer? In the past, I have witnessed the confirmations of God when I taught the Faith, and there have been many. I remember confirmations in my marriage, too! What a bounty I have experienced! I will bring them to mind when I feel unworthy or feel like giving up.

Reflection: Bahá'u'lláh has cautioned in the Hidden Words, "Withdraw your hands from tyranny for I have pledged Myself not to forgive any man's injustice." However, in the verse above, He indicates that if I truly repent and return to him, He will forgive my trespasses. What idle fancies prevent me from repenting and asking for His mercy and forgiveness? What idle fancies prevent me from forgiving myself after I have repented? Have I forgiven my spouse?

Faithful

Reflection: In the first quotation of this chapter, Bahá'u'lláh states that there are foolish ones who have been "nurtured in evil passions and desires!" This sounds very much like the fact that I was nurtured as a child in sexual behaviors! No wonder Bahá'u'lláh continually speaks of God's mercy and forgiveness. I was very foolish in the past and the only way I was enabled to change my behavior was by being alert to the lessons God provided for me.

– *Notes* –

Meditation 19

Am I a Bahá'í in Name Only?

Idle Fancies and Vain Imaginings

"Blessed art thou and blessed is the mother that hath nursed thee. Appreciate the value of this station and arise to serve His Cause in such wise that the idle fancies and insinuations of the doubters withhold thee not from this high resolve. The Day-Star of certitude is shining resplendent but the people of the world are holding fast unto vain imaginings. The Ocean of divine knowledge hath risen high whilst the children of men are clinging to the hem of the foolish. But for the unfailing grace of God – exalted be His glory – no antidote could ever cure these inveterate diseases." — Baha'u'llah.[157]

Spotless Chastity

"Say: He is not to be numbered with the people of Bahá who followeth his mundane desires, or fixeth his heart on things of the earth. He is My true follower who, if he come to a valley of pure gold, will pass straight through it aloof as a cloud, and will neither turn back, nor pause. Such a man is, assuredly, of Me. From his garment the Concourse on high can inhale the fragrance of sanctity.... And if he met the fairest and most comely of women, he would not feel his heart seduced by the least shadow of desire for her beauty. Such an one, indeed, is the creation of spotless chastity. Thus instructeth you the Pen of the Ancient of Days, as bidden by your Lord, the Almighty, the All-Bountiful." — Baha'u'llah[158]

Prayer for Forgiveness and Mercy

"I am he, O my Lord, that hath confessed to Thee the multitude of his evil doings, that hath acknowledged what no man hath acknowledged. I have made haste to attain unto the ocean of Thy forgiveness, and have sought shelter beneath the shadow of Thy most gracious favor. Grant, I beseech Thee, O Thou Who art the Everlasting King and the Sovereign Protector of all men, that I may be enabled to manifest that which shall cause the hearts and souls of men to soar in the limitless immensity of Thy love, and to commune with Thy Spirit. Strengthen me through the power of Thy sovereignty, that I may turn all created things towards the Day Spring of Thy Manifestation and the Source of Thy Revelation. Aid me, O my Lord, to surrender myself wholly to Thy Will, and to arise and serve Thee, for I cherish this earthly life for no other purpose than to compass the Tabernacle of Thy Revelation and the Seat of Thy Glory. Thou seest me, O my God, detached from all else but Thee, and humble and subservient to Thy Will. Deal with me as it beseemeth Thee, and as it befitteth Thy highness and great glory."
— Baha'u'llah[159]

Nobility of Man

"You must thank God that your efforts are high and noble, that your endeavors are worthy, that your intentions are centered upon the Kingdom of God and that your supreme desire is the acquisition of eternal virtues. You must act in accordance with these requirements. A man may be a Bahá'í in name only. If he is a Bahá'í in reality, his deeds and actions will be decisive proofs of it. What are the requirements? Love for mankind, sincerity toward all, reflecting the oneness of the world of humanity, philanthropy, becoming enkindled with the fire of the love of God, attainment to the knowledge of God and that which is conducive to human welfare." — 'Abdu'l-Baha[160]

Praise Be to God

"Praise be to God! The springtime of God is at hand. This century is verily the spring season. The world of mind and the kingdom of soul have become fresh and verdant by its bestowals. It has resuscitated the whole realm of existence. On one hand the lights of reality are shining; on the other the clouds of divine mercy are pouring down the fullness of heavenly bounty. Wonderful material progress is evident and great spiritual discoveries are being made. Truly this can be called the miracle of centuries for it is replete with manifestations of the miraculous. The time has come when all mankind shall be united, when all races shall be loyal to one fatherland, all religions become one religion and racial and religious bias pass away. It is a day in which the oneness of humankind shall uplift its standard and international peace like the true morning flood the world with its light. Therefore we offer supplications to God, asking him to dispel these gloomy clouds and uproot these imitations in order that the East and West may become radiant with love and unity; that the nations of the world shall embrace each other and the ideal spiritual brotherhood illumine the world like the glorious sun of the high heavens."
— 'Abdu'l-Baha[161]

Reflection: If I am a Bahá'í in reality, my deeds and noble actions for the welfare of the world will be the decisive proofs of it. How can I show more love for mankind, more love for people of other religions and more gratefulness for the Divine Unity of all the Prophets, while becoming more and more detached from my idle fancies and vain imaginings?

Faithful

Reflection: The first Tablet in this chapter was originally written for the handmaidens. Bahá'u'lláh speaks of the Ocean of divine knowledge and compares it to vain imaginings. There is no other antidote that could cure these inveterate diseases and steer me away from my mundane desires. Do a brief inventory of the vain imaginings that the world condones and that in comparison with the instructions of God would be considered foolish, inveterate diseases. Make a list of immoral practices that the world condones and that lead our youth astray. Compare also a moment of certitude that has bestowed insight and created a higher resolve.

Bahá'í Youth

"Even though the Bahá'í youth should feel with the condition in which they see their non-Bahá'í friends and not indict them for it, they should not let themselves be carried by the wave of world events as they are being carried. Whereas they see before them only a world that is crumbling down we are also seeing a new world being built up. Whereas they experience the destruction of old institutions that commanded their respect, we are beholding the dawn of a new era with its strict commands and new social bonds. Their materialistic outlook shows them the futility of all things while our faith in a regenerated and spiritualized man makes us look to the future and build for it. To make them follow our ways we should sympathize with their plight but should not follow their ways. We should take our stand on a higher plane of moral and spiritual life and, setting for them the true example, urge them up to our level. The young people should read what Bahá'u'lláh and the Master say on such matters and follow them conscientiously. That is if they desire to be true to the teachings and establish them throughout the world." — Shoghi Effendi[162]

Meditation 20

May all the Latent Fragrant Flowers in My Heart Become Reality

Idle Fancies and Vain Imaginings
"O SON OF MAN!
"The light hath shone on thee from the horizon of the sacred Mount and the spirit of enlightenment hath breathed in the Sinai of thy heart. Wherefore, free thyself from the veils of idle fancies and enter into My court, that thou mayest be fit for everlasting life and worthy to meet Me. Thus may death not come upon thee, neither weariness nor trouble."   — Baha'u'llah[163]

Purity and Chastity
"You must become the lamps of Bahá'u'lláh so that you may shine with eternal light and be the proofs and evidences of His truth. Then will such signs of purity and chastity be witnessed in your deeds and actions that men will behold the heavenly radiance of your lives and say, 'Verily, ye are the proofs of Bahá'u'lláh. Verily, Bahá'u'lláh is the True One, for He has trained such souls as these, each one of which is a proof in himself.' They will say to others, 'Come and witness the conduct of these souls; come and listen to their words, behold the illumination of their hearts, see the evidences of the love of God in them, consider their praiseworthy morals, and discover the foundations of the oneness of humanity firmly implanted within them. What greater proof can there be than these people that the message of Bahá'u'lláh is truth and reality?' It is my hope that each one of you shall be a herald of God, proclaiming the evidences of His appearance, in words, deeds and thoughts.

Faithful

Let your actions and utterances be a witness that you are of the Kingdom of Bahá'u'lláh. These are the duties enjoined upon you by Bahá'u'lláh." — 'Abdu'l-Baha[164]

Prayer for Forgiveness and Mercy

"I am but a poor creature, O my Lord; I have clung to the hem of Thy riches. I am sore sick; I have held fast the cord of Thy healing. Deliver me from the ills that have encircled me, and wash me thoroughly with the waters of Thy graciousness and mercy, and attire me with the raiment of wholesomeness, through Thy forgiveness and bounty. Fix, then, mine eyes upon Thee, and rid me of all attachment to aught else except Thyself. Aid me to do what Thou desirest, and to fulfill what Thou pleasest.

"Thou art truly the Lord of this life and of the next. Thou art, in truth, the Ever-Forgiving, the Most Merciful." — Baha'u'llah[165]

Nobility of Man

"O SON OF BOUNTY! Out of the wastes of nothingness, with the clay of My command I made thee to appear, and have ordained for thy training every atom in existence and the essence of all created things. Thus, ere thou didst issue from thy mother's womb, I destined for thee two founts of gleaming milk, eyes to watch over thee, and hearts to love thee. Out of My loving-kindness, 'neath the shade of My mercy I nurtured thee, and guarded thee by the essence of My grace and favor. And My purpose in all this was that thou mightest attain My everlasting dominion and become worthy of My invisible bestowals. And yet heedless thou didst remain, and when fully grown, thou didst neglect all My bounties and occupied thyself with thine idle imaginings, in such wise that thou didst become wholly forgetful, and, turning away from the portals of the Friend didst abide within the courts of My enemy." — Baha'u'llah [165.5]

Remaining

"Man is a child of God, most noble, lofty and beloved by God, his Creator. Therefore, he must ever strive that the divine bounties and virtues bestowed upon him may prevail and control him. Just now the soil of human hearts seems like black earth, but in the innermost substance of this dark soil there are thousands of fragrant flowers latent. We must endeavor to cultivate and awaken these potentialities, discover the secret treasure in this very mine and depository of God, bring forth these resplendent powers long hidden in human hearts. Then will the glories of both worlds be blended and increased and the quintessence of human existence be made manifest."
— 'Abdu'l-Baha[166]

Praise Be to God
"The holy Manifestations of God come into the world to dispel the darkness of the animal or physical nature of man, to purify him from his imperfections in order that his heavenly and spiritual nature may become quickened, his divine qualities awakened, his perfections visible, his potential powers revealed and all the virtues of the world of humanity latent within him may come to life. These holy Manifestations of God are the educators and trainers of the world of existence, the teachers of the world of humanity. They liberate man from the darkness of the world of nature, deliver him from despair, error, ignorance, imperfections and all evil qualities. They clothe him in the garment of perfections and exalted virtues. Men are ignorant; the Manifestations of God make them wise. They are animalistic; the Manifestations make them human. They are savage and cruel; the Manifestations lead them into kingdoms of light and love. They are unjust; the Manifestations cause them to become just. Man is selfish; they sever him from self and desire. Man is haughty; they make him meek, humble and friendly. He is earthly; they make him heavenly. Men are

material; the Manifestations transform them into semblance divine. They are immature children; the Manifestations develop them into maturity. Man is poor; they endow him with wealth. Man is base, treacherous and mean; the Manifestations of God uplift him into dignity, nobility and loftiness. — 'Abdu'l-Baha[167]

Reflection: As I polish my mirror it will shine with eternal life and the veil of idle fancies will be removed. The weariness of my busy, busy mind will cease in the presence of certitude and assurance. "Grant that I may become confirmed in my allegiance to Thy Faith, and bestow upon me a fuller measure of certitude and assurance, that I may wholly dispense with the world..." 'Abdu'l-Baha[168] "Most of the people are enwrapped in fancy and idle imaginings: Where are the exponents of Thy certitude, O Assurance of the worlds?" Baha'u'llah[169] To gain certitude right now, I will write out moments of certitude I have received in the past. This will make His Kingdom real to me.

Reflection: God has granted nobility upon me. He nurtured me when I was unable to care for myself. How can I raise my thoughts to make them more lofty with each passing day so that instead of being forgetful and turning away from the Friend, I become the means of spreading His light to all men? 'Abdu'l-Bahá says that though the soil of my heart is dark, that there are thousands of latent fragrant flowers there. May I strive to bring them out of darkness by reading His word daily. I love the concept that there are latent fragrant flowers that equate with my future deeds of purity.

Meditation 21

The Goals are Insight and Detachment, Vision and Upliftment!

Idle Fancies and Vain Imaginings
"This is not a Cause which may be made a plaything for your idle fancies, nor is it a field for the foolish and faint of heart. By God, this is the arena of insight and detachment, of vision and upliftment, where none may spur on their chargers save the valiant horsemen of the Merciful, who have severed all attachment to the world of being. These, truly, are they that render God victorious on earth, and are the dawning-places of His sovereign might amidst mankind." — Baha'u'llah[170]

Faithfulness and Chastity
"In brief, let each one of you be as a lamp shining forth with the light of the virtues of the world of humanity. Be trustworthy, sincere, affectionate and replete with chastity. Be illumined, be spiritual, be divine, be glorious, be quickened of God, be a Bahá'í" — 'Abdu'l-Baha[171]

Prayer for Forgiveness and Mercy
"Glory be to Thee, O Lord my God! I beg of Thee by Thy Name through which He Who is Thy Beauty hath been stablished upon the throne of Thy Cause, and by Thy Name through which Thou changest all things, and gatherest together all things, and callest to account all things, and rewardest all things, and preservest all things, and sustainest all things – I beg of Thee to guard this handmaiden who hath fled for refuge to Thee, and hath sought the shelter of Him in Whom Thou Thyself art manifest, and hath put her whole trust and confidence in Thee.

"She is sick, O my God, and hath entered beneath the shadow of the Tree of Thy healing; afflicted, and hath fled to the City of Thy protection; diseased, and hath sought the Fountain-Head of Thy favors; sorely vexed, and hath hasted to attain the Well-Spring of Thy tranquility; burdened with sin, and hath set her face toward the court of Thy forgiveness.

"Attire her, by Thy sovereignty and Thy loving-kindness, O my God and my Beloved, with the raiment of Thy balm and Thy healing, and make her quaff of the cup of Thy mercy and Thy favors. Protect her, moreover, from every affliction and ailment, from all pain and sickness, and from whatsoever may be abhorrent unto Thee.

"Thou, in truth, art immensely exalted above all else except Thyself. Thou art, verily, the Healer, the All-Sufficing, the Preserver, the Ever-Forgiving, the Most Merciful." — Baha'u'llah[172]

Nobility of Man

"In the world of existence there is nothing so important as spirit, nothing so essential as the spirit of man. The spirit of man is the most noble of phenomena. The spirit of man is the meeting between man and God. The spirit of man is the animus of human life and the collective center of all human virtues. The spirit of man is the cause of the illumination of this world. The world may be likened to the body; man is the spirit of the body, because the light of the world is the human spirit. Man is the life of the world, and the life of man is the spirit. The happiness of the world depends upon man, and the happiness of man is dependent upon the spirit. The world may be likened to the lamp chimney, whereas man is the light. Man himself may be likened to the lamp; his spirit is the light within the lamp." ' — Abdu'l-Baha[173]

Praise Be to God

"O My servant that hath turned thy face towards Me! Render thanks unto God for having sent down unto thee this Tablet in this Prison, that thou mayest remind the people of the days of thy Lord, the All-Glorious, the All-Knowing. Thus have We established for thee, through the waters of Our wisdom and utterance, the foundations of thy belief. This, verily, is the water whereon the Throne of thy Lord hath been raised. "His Throne had stood upon the waters." Ponder this in thine heart, that thou mayest comprehend its meaning. Say: Praise be to God, the Lord of all worlds." — Baha'u'llah[174]

– Notes –

Reflection: God is an Unknowable Essence Who has bestowed His Revelation upon Bahá'u'lláh, that I might know God and render Him victorious on earth. It is unseemly of me as a noble servant to treat the Cause as a plaything for my idle fancies. *"32. O BEFRIENDED STRANGER! The candle of thine heart is lighted by the hand of My power, quench it not with the contrary winds of self and passion. The healer of all thine ills is remembrance of Me, forget it not. Make My love thy treasure and cherish it even as thy very sight and life."* Baha'u'llah [175] What does it mean to remember God and cherish His love for me, instead of acting foolish and being faint of heart?

Reflection: There are many forms of sickness. Immorality is one, idle fancies and vain imaginings are another... drugs and alcohol... sexual addiction... pornography. They are abhorrent to God and are not in keeping with His desire that I maintain my noble station. When I am sorely vexed by my behavior, what do I turn to, comfort food, romantic notions, or other addictions? What could I trade these behaviors for? I can write them out. I don't have to show them to anyone.

— *Notes* —

Meditation 22

The Raiment of the Human Heart is the Fear of God

Idle Fancies and Vain Imaginings

"Praise be unto Thee, O our God, that Thou hast sent down unto us that which draweth us nigh unto Thee, and supplieth us with every good thing sent down by Thee in Thy Books and Thy Scriptures. Protect us, we beseech Thee, O my Lord, from the hosts of idle fancies and vain imaginations. Thou, in truth, art the Mighty, the All-Knowing." — Baha'u'llah[176]

Faithfulness and Chastity

"Entrance into the Kingdom is through the love of God, through detachment, through holiness and chastity, through truthfulness, purity, steadfastness, faithfulness and the sacrifice of life.

"These explanations show that man is immortal and lives eternally. For those who believe in God, who have love of God, and faith, life is excellent – that is, it is eternal; but to those souls who are veiled from God, although they have life, it is dark, and in comparison with the life of believers it is nonexistence." — 'Abdu'l-Baha[177]

Prayer for Forgiveness and Healing

"Glory be to Thee, O Lord my God! I implore Thee by Thy Name, through which Thou didst lift up the ensigns of Thy guidance, and didst shed the radiance of Thy loving-kindness, and didst reveal the sovereignty of Thy Lordship; through which the lamp of Thy names hath appeared within the niche of Thine attributes, and He Who is the Tabernacle of Thy unity and the Manifestation of detachment hath shone forth; through which the ways of Thy guidance were made known, and the paths of Thy good pleasure were marked out; through which the foundations of error have been made to tremble, and *the signs of wickedness have been abolished; through which the fountains of wisdom have burst forth, and the heavenly table hath been sent down; through which Thou didst preserve Thy servants and didst vouchsafe Thy healing; through which Thou didst show forth Thy tender mercies unto Thy servants and revealedst Thy forgiveness amidst Thy creatures – I implore Thee to keep safe him who hath held fast and returned unto Thee, and clung to Thy mercy, and seized the hem of Thy loving providence. Send down, then, upon him Thy healing, and make him whole, and endue him with a constancy vouchsafed by Thee, and a tranquility bestowed by Thy highness.*

Thou art, verily, the Healer, the Preserver, the Helper, the Almighty, the Powerful, the All-Glorious, the All-Knowing." — Baha'u'llah[178]

Nobility of Man

"Altogether it is evident that man is more noble and superior, that in him there is an ideal power surpassing nature. He has consciousness, volition, memory, intelligent power, divine attributes and virtues of which nature is completely deprived and bereft; therefore, man is higher and nobler by reason of the ideal and heavenly force latent and manifest in him." — 'Abdu'l-Baha[179]

Praise Be to God

"The spirit that animateth the human heart is the

knowledge of God, and its truest adorning is the recognition of the truth that "He doeth whatsoever He willeth, and ordaineth that which He pleaseth." Its raiment is the fear of God, and its perfection steadfastness in His Faith. Thus God instructeth whosoever seeketh Him. He, verily, loveth the one that turneth towards Him. There is none other God but Him, the Forgiving, the Most Bountiful. All praise be to God, the Lord of all worlds."

— *Baha'u'llah*[180]

Reflection: Do you think Bahá'u'lláh would put this prayer for protection in the Long Obligatory Prayer if

Faithful

He didn't know we would be challenged by idle fancies and vain imaginations daily? I have to give up the idea that I am the "only one" who has idle fancies and vain imaginations!! How can honesty with my spouse improve my marriage or relationships? A counselor or therapist can recognize when a client is not being honest with their spouse. Truthfulness is a virtue, which is the basis of honesty. Denial destroys trust. It is difficult to improve relationships when instead of getting honesty, we get denial or evasiveness. We cannot get at the heart of the problem when we are in denial or in a state of distrust.

Reflection: The healing prayer above is key to forgiveness for those who return to God. It's not just for healing from a physical illness. By praying this prayer I am asking God to put me through a series of lessons that will open my eyes and ears and make me whole and constant and tranquil. I am worthy of this. What would make me want to be faithful to my family? I have an ideal power that surpasses my nature. It's inherent and can be called upon! It is my inherent nobility!

– *Notes* –

Meditation 23

Fulfilling God's Purpose on Earth

Idle Fancies and Vain Imaginings

"The day is approaching when God will have, by an act of His Will, raised up a race of men the nature of which is inscrutable to all save God, the All-Powerful, the Self-Subsisting. He shall purify them from the defilement of idle fancies and corrupt desires, shall lift them up to the heights of holiness, and shall cause them to manifest the signs of His sovereignty and might upon earth. Thus hath it been ordained by God, the All-Glorious, the All-Loving." — Baha'u'llah[181]

Faithfulness and Chastity

"This gathering must be completely spiritual. That is, the discussions must be confined to marshalling clear and conclusive proofs that the Sun of Truth hath indeed arisen. And further, those present should concern themselves with every means of training the girl children; with teaching the various branches of knowledge, good behaviour, a proper way of life, the cultivation of a good character, chastity and constancy, perseverance, strength, determination, firmness of purpose; with household management, the education of children, and whatever especially applieth to the needs of girls – to the end that these girls, reared in the stronghold of all perfections, and with the protection of a goodly character, will, when they themselves become mothers, bring up their children from earliest infancy to have a good character and conduct themselves well."
— 'Abdu'l-Baha[182]

Prayer for Forgiveness, Mercy and Grace

"O Thou Who art the All-Knowing! Wayward though

we be, we still cling to Thy bounty; and though ignorant, we still set our faces toward the ocean of Thy wisdom. Thou art that All-Bountiful Who art not deterred by a multitude of sins from vouchsafing Thy bounty, and the flow of Whose gifts is not arrested by the withdrawal of the peoples of the world. From eternity the door of Thy grace hath remained wide open. A dewdrop out of the ocean of Thy mercy is able to adorn all things with the ornament of sanctity, and a sprinkling of the waters of Thy bounty can cause the entire creation to attain unto true wealth.

"Lift not the veil, O Thou Who art the Concealer! From eternity the tokens of Thy bounty have encompassed the universe, and the splendors of Thy Most Great Name have been shed over all created things. Deny not Thy servants the wonders of Thy grace. Cause them to be made aware of Thee, that they may bear witness to Thy unity, and enable them to recognize Thee, that they may hasten towards Thee. Thy mercy hath embraced the whole creation, and Thy grace hath pervaded all things. From the billows of the ocean of Thy generosity the seas of eagerness and enthusiasm were revealed. Thou art what Thou art. Aught except Thee is unworthy of any mention unless it entereth beneath Thy shadow, and gaineth admittance into Thy court.

"Whatever betide us, we beseech Thine ancient forgiveness, and seek Thine all-pervasive grace. Our hope is that Thou wilt deny no one Thy grace, and wilt deprive no soul of the ornament of fairness and justice. Thou art the King of all bounty, and the Lord of all favors, and supreme over all who are in heaven and on earth." — Baha'u'llah[183]

Nobility of Man

"The noblest of men is he who serves humankind, and he is nearest the threshold of God who is the least of His servants. The glory and majesty of man are dependent upon his servitude to his fellow creatures and not upon the exercise of hostility and hatred." — 'Abdu'l-Baha[186]

Praise Be to God

"Verily I say, in this most mighty Revelation, all the Dispensations of the past have attained their highest, their final consummation. Thus counselleth you your Lord, the All-Knowing, the All-Wise. Praise be to God, the Lord of all worlds." — Baha'u'llah[187]

— Notes —

Reflection: Adultery isn't the only issue we have idle fancies and corrupt desires for. In the past I have wanted fame, at times I have felt wanton as far as material things are considered, and still at other times I have felt like flotsam on the shores of Bahá'u'lláh's ocean because I had been roving distracted with no true goal. Yet returning to God in repentance lifts me up "to the heights of holiness." In the following passage 'Abdu'l-Bahá directs me as to how I can fulfill God's purpose on earth. Where do I fit in in accomplishing these spiritual goals?

Reflection: I may be wayward and ignorant, yet God is not deterred by my sins and continues to shower me with bounties. I have an obligation to my family to serve them (and my Lord) with glory and majesty, rather than modeling hostility and hatred. It's not too late to reconstruct the foundation of my relationship to my spouse. Genuflecting to God is a first step. Marriage counseling is a second step.

"Consultation is…available for the individual in solving his own problems; he may consult with his Assembly, with his family and with his friends."
— Universal House of Justice[184]

"Neither you nor your husband should hesitate to continue consulting professional marriage counselors, individually and together if possible, and also to take advantage of the supportive counseling which can come from wise and mature friends. Non-Bahá'í counseling can be useful but it is usually necessary to temper it with Bahá'í insight." — Universal House of Justice[185]

Meditation 24

How Much Am I Prepared to Sacrifice?
How Sincere Am I?

Idle Fancies and Vain Imaginings

"We, verily, have ordained this Temple to be the source of all existence in the new creation, that all may know of a certainty My power to accomplish that which I have purposed through My word "Be", and it is! Beneath the shadow of every letter of this Temple We shall raise up a people whose number none can reckon save God, the Help in Peril, the Self-Subsisting. Erelong shall God bring forth from His Temple such souls as will remain unswayed by the insinuations of the rebellious, and who will quaff at all times of the cup that is life indeed. These, truly, are of the blissful.

"These souls are the protectors of the Cause of God on earth, who shall preserve its beauty from the obscuring dust of idle fancies and vain imaginings. In the path of their Lord they shall not fear for their lives; rather will they sacrifice their all in their eagerness to behold the face of their Well-Beloved when once He hath appeared in this Name, the Almighty, the All-Powerful, the All-Glorious, the Most Holy." — Baha'u'llah[188]

Faithfulness and Chastity

"Shams-i-Duha remained in Isfahan. She spent her days and nights in the remembrance of God and in teaching His Cause to the women of that city. She was gifted with an eloquent tongue; her utterance was wonderful to hear. She was highly honored by the leading women of Isfahan, celebrated for piety, for godliness, and the

purity of her life. She was chastity embodied; all her hours were spent in reciting Holy Writ, or expounding the Texts, or unraveling the most complex of spiritual themes, or spreading abroad the sweet savors of God."
'Abdu'l-Baha[189]

Prayer for Forgiveness and Mercy

"Praise be unto Thee, Who art my God and the God of all men, and my Desire and the Desire of all them that have recognized Thee, and my Beloved and the Beloved of such as have acknowledged Thy unity, and the Object of my adoration and of the adoration of them that have near access to Thee, and my Wish and the Wish of such as are wholly devoted to Thee, and my Hope and the Hope of them that have fixed their hearts upon Thee, and my Refuge and the Refuge of all such as have hastened towards Thee, and my Haven and the Haven of whosoever hath repaired unto Thee, and my Goal and the Goal of all them that have set themselves towards Thee, and my Object and the Object of those who have fixed their gaze upon Thee, and my Paradise and the Paradise of them that have ascended towards Thee, and my Lode-star and the Lode-star of all such as yearn after Thee, and my Joy and the Joy of all them that love Thee, and my Light and the Light of all such as have erred and asked to be forgiven by Thee, and my Exultation and the Exultation of all them that remember Thee, and my Stronghold and the Stronghold of all such as have fled to Thee, and my Sanctuary and the Sanctuary of all that dread Thee, and my Lord and the Lord of all such as dwell in the heavens and on the earth!"

— Baha'u'llah[190]

Nobility of Man

"According to the words of the Old Testament God has said, "Let us make man in our image, after our likeness." This indicates that man is of the image and likeness of God – that is to say, the perfections of God, the divine virtues, are reflected or revealed in the human reality. Just as the light and effulgence of the sun when cast upon a polished mirror are reflected fully, gloriously, so, likewise, the qualities and attributes of Divinity are radiated from the depths of a pure human heart. This is an evidence that man is the most noble of God's creatures." — 'Abdu'l-Baha[191]

Praise Be to God

"All praise be to God Who hath adorned the world with an ornament, and arrayed it with a vesture, of which it can be despoiled by no earthly power, however mighty its battalions, however vast its wealth, however profound its influence. Say: the essence of all power is God's, the highest and the last End of all creation. The source of all majesty is God's, the Object of the adoration of all that is in the heavens and all that is on the earth. Such forces as have their origin in this world of dust are, by their very nature, unworthy of consideration."
— Baha'u'llah[192]

Reflection: Can I reach for Bahá'u'lláh's Revelation in my state of rebelliousness? It is my understanding that the Temple referred to in the first quotation of this meditation is His Revelation and it can lead me to the "snow white path." Those who quaff of this cup He has revealed will be of the blissful. This is not something to be taken lightly. Man or woman, I can use the Bahá'í woman, Shams-i-Duha, as a model for behavior fitting a servant of God. Are my idle fancies and vain imaginings born of the "models" that are sanctioned by the world or a social reality that does not begin to equate with a Bahá'í model? Who were my models before I became a Bahá'í? What is my model now?

Reflection: God is indeed my Refuge, Sanctuary and Stronghold who I can turn to for forgiveness, grace and mercy. Miracles happen every day when His Revelation is reflected in our human reality. This is what purifies my heart. What evidence do I see in others and myself that man is the most noble of God's creatures?

— Notes —

Meditation 25

Tarry Not!

Idle Fancies and Vain Imaginings

"Say: Take heed lest your devotions withhold you from Him Who is the object of all devotion, or your worship debar you from Him Who is the object of all worship. Rend asunder the veils of your idle fancies! This is your Lord, the Almighty, the All-Knowing, Who hath come to quicken the world and unite all who dwell on earth. Turn unto the Dayspring of Revelation, O people, and tarry not, be it for less than the twinkling of an eye. Read ye the Evangel and yet refuse to acknowledge the All-Glorious Lord? This indeed beseemeth you not, O concourse of learned men!

"Say: If ye deny this Revelation, by what proof have ye believed in God? Produce it then. Thus hath the summons of God been sent down by the Pen of the Most High at the bidding of your Lord, the Most Glorious, in this Tablet from whose horizon the splendour of His Light hath shone forth. How many are My servants whose deeds have become veils between them and their own selves, and who have been kept back thereby from drawing nigh unto God, He Who causeth the winds to blow."

— Baha'u'llah[193]

Chastity, Faithfulness

"O saints of God! At the end of Our discourse We enjoin on you once again chastity, faithfulness, godliness, sincerity, and purity. Lay aside the evil and adopt the good. This is that whereunto ye are commanded in the Book of God, the Knowing, the Wise. Well is it with those who practice [this injunction]. At this moment the pen crieth out, saying, 'O saints of God, regard the horizon of uprightness, and be quit, severed, and free from what is beside this. There is no strength and no power save in God." — 'Abdu'l-Baha[194]

Prayer for Forgiveness and Mercy

"O Thou in separation from Whom hearts and souls have melted, and by the fire of Whose love the whole world hath been set aflame! I implore Thee by Thy Name through which Thou hast subdued the whole creation, not to withhold from me that which is with Thee, O Thou Who rulest over all men! Thou seest, O my Lord, this stranger hastening to his most exalted home beneath the canopy of Thy majesty and within the precincts of Thy mercy; and this transgressor seeking the ocean of Thy forgiveness; and this lowly one the court of Thy glory; and this poor creature the orient of Thy wealth. Thine is the authority to command whatsoever Thou willest. I bear witness that Thou art to be praised in Thy doings, and to be obeyed in Thy behests, and to remain unconstrained in Thy bidding." — Baha'u'llah[195]

Nobility of Man

"The reason of the mission of the Prophets is to educate men, so that this piece of coal may become a diamond, and this fruitless tree may be engrafted and yield the sweetest, most delicious fruits. When man reaches the noblest state in the world of humanity, then he can make further progress in the conditions of perfection, but not in state; for such states are limited, but the divine perfections are endless." — 'Abdu'l-Baha[196]

Praise Be to God

"I am the one, O my Lord, who hath held fast the cord of Thy loving-kindness, and clung to the hem of Thy mercy and favors. Do Thou ordain for me and for my loved ones the good of this world and of the world to come. Supply them, then, with the Hidden Gift Thou didst ordain for the choicest among Thy creatures.

"These are, O my Lord, the days in which Thou hast bidden Thy servants to observe the fast. Blessed is he that observeth the fast wholly for Thy sake and with absolute detachment from all things except Thee. Assist me and assist them, O my Lord, to obey Thee and to keep Thy precepts. Thou, verily, hast power to do what Thou choosest.

"There is no God but Thee, the All-Knowing, the All-Wise. All praise be to God, the Lord of all worlds." Baha'u'llah[197]

Reflection: Honesty with oneself is necessary to rend asunder the veils of idle fancies." Monitoring my thoughts and deeds is part of bringing myself to account for my actions. Bahá'u'lláh instructs all of us to tarry not. Again, this is a process of becoming aware. What is it in Bahá'u'lláh's Revelation that leads me to "Lay aside the evil and adopt the good?"

Reflection: When I pray the prayer in this chapter, I am literally begging for God's ocean of forgiveness and admitting my lowly state. This is more self honesty and it's the state of all on earth, for we are all progressing in a state toward perfection. Though I know I am not the only one, I take heart that my station is high because I have been created noble as all human beings are; and I take my spiritual education seriously! The Master zeros in on the need to educate men so they will yield the sweetest fruits. How has Bahá'u'lláh's Revelation educated me with His principles? Isn't chastity just another step toward perfection?

Reflection: The heavens of men's idle fancies and vain imaginations is a "lala land" that has to be split asunder. And the Word of God does that for me if I am steadfast in keeping my part of God's Covenant which requires me to meditate on it daily. It is the fear of God that drives me to educate myself and give up my corrupt desires. What is the price of nobility for me? What would I eliminate from my life in order to please God?

Reflection: The following quotation is from my book "Healing the Wounded Soul, "There are fine nuances between our biological response and our romantic feelings, but one who is spiritually discerning can separate his or her biological response from the fact that this indeed is a moment of conscious choice to remain within the boundaries of the laws of God. Keith Clark, a priest, tells us, "Sometimes a celibate is affected romantically and genitally by the relationships he or she has with others, but romance and genital activity are not pursued." He adds, "The unique demands of religious life do not dictate what a celibate feels and experiences, but they do determine the behaviors we can choose and the kind of relationships we can form as a result of those behaviors." Keith Clark[198]

Reflection: Oh, the wisdom of prayer for a humble servant of God! There is no shame in confessing to God that I have trespassed and strayed. But voicing it is not the hardest part, it is believing that God's mercy and grace far exceeds my short comings and that He will make known to me a miraculous path to nobility. Who knows your journey towards perfection better than God? Never lose hope! For 'Abdu'l-Bahá advises:

"Never lose thy trust in God! Be thou ever hopeful for the bounties of God never cease to flow upon man. If viewed from one perspective, they seem to decrease. But from another, they are full and complete. Man is under all conditions immersed in sea of God's blessings. Therefore, be thou not hopeless under any circumstances, but rather be firm in thy hope."

— *'Abdu'l-Baha*[199]

Faithful

- *Notes* -

Last Thoughts

Man as the Supreme Talisman

Man is the supreme Talisman. Lack of a proper education hath, however, deprived him of that which he doth inherently possess. Through a word proceeding out of the mouth of God he was called into being; by one word more he was guided to recognize the Source of his education; by yet another word his station and destiny were safeguarded. The Great Being saith: Regard man as a mine rich in gems of inestimable value. Education can, alone, cause it to reveal its treasures, and enable mankind to benefit therefrom. If any man were to meditate on that which the Scriptures, sent down from the heaven of God's holy Will, have revealed, he would readily recognize that their purpose is that all men shall be regarded as one soul, so that the seal bearing the words "The Kingdom shall be God's" may be stamped on every heart, and the light of Divine bounty, of grace, and mercy may envelop all mankind. The one true God, exalted be His glory, hath wished nothing for Himself. The allegiance of mankind profiteth Him not, neither doth its perversity harm Him. The Bird of the Realm of Utterance voiceth continually this call: "All things have I willed for thee, and thee, too, for thine own sake." If the learned and worldly-wise men of this age were to allow mankind to inhale the fragrance of fellowship and love, every understanding heart would apprehend the meaning of true liberty, and discover the secret of undisturbed peace and absolute composure. Were the earth to attain this station and be illumined with its light it could then be truly said of it: "Thou shall see in it no hollows or rising hills."

— Baha'u'llah[200]

The Station of Man

"We hold firmly the conviction that all human beings have been created "to carry forward an ever-advancing civilization"; that "to act like the beasts of the field is unworthy of man"; that the virtues that befit human dignity are trustworthiness, forbearance, mercy, compassion and loving-kindness towards all peoples. We reaffirm the belief that the "potentialities inherent in the station of man, the full measure of his destiny on earth, the innate excellence of his reality, must all be manifested in this promised Day of God." These are the motivations for our unshakeable faith that unity and peace are the attainable goal towards which humanity is striving." — *Universal House of Justice*[201]

Reflection: Prior to writing this book I had no idea how valuable it would be to me and how much my character flaws would be helped by it. I turn to it as my meditation in the morning, in the evening and before I go to bed at midnight. I have no other choice if I want to live the life. It is crucial for that undeveloped part of me. I pray that others might be helped by its simplicity

May God guide you in paths of restfulness and peace!

APPENDIX

Additional Resources for the Reader

Books on Infidelity and for Troubled Marriages

The Divorce Remedy: The Proven 7-Step Program for Saving Your Marriage, Michele Weiner Davis

NOT "Just Friends", Shirley Glass, Ph.D.

Staying Together When an Affair Pulls You Apart, Stephen M. Judah, Ph.D.

Surviving an Affair, Dr. Willard F. Harley, Jr. and Dr. Jennifer Harley Chalmers

My Husband's Affair Became the Best Thing That Ever Happened to Me, Anne Bercht

Unfaithful, Rebuilding Trust After Infidelity, Gary & Mona Shriver

Torn Asunder, Recovering from Extramarital Affairs, Dave Carder

You Can't Have Him—He's Mine, Marie H. Browne, R.N., Ph.D.

Avoiding the Greener Grass Syndrome, How to Grow Affair-Proof Hedges Around Your Marriage, Nancy C. Anderson

To Have and to Hold, Peggy Vaughan

Online Marital Protection and Infidelity
   Facebook and Your Marriage, K. Jason & Kelli Krafsky, www.fbmarriage.com/

Books on Marriage Building

Fighting for Your Marriage, Howard J. Markman, Scott M. Stanley, Susan L. Blumberg

Hold Me Tight, Dr. Sue Johnson

Pure Gold: Encouraging Character Qualities in Marriage, Susanne M. Alexander with Craig A. Farnsworth and John S. Miller (contains interfaith content, including Bahá'í quotations)
A selection at:
www.marriagetransformation.com/Baháí.htm;
www.smartmarriages.com; or www.healthymarriageinfo.org

Books on Separation and Reconciliation

Taking Space, How to Use Separation to Explore the Future of Your Relationship, Robert J. Buchicchio

Hope for the Separated, Wounded Marriages Can Be Healed, Gary Chapman

Should I Stay or Go? How Controlled Separation Can Save Your Marriage, Lee Raffel

Websites
- www.smartmarriages.com
- www.marriagebuilders.com
- www.affairrecovery.com/
- www.divorcebusting.com
- www.beyondaffairs.com

Sexual Addiction: www.faithfulandtrueministries.com
Bahá'í Faith: www.Baháimarriage.net

References:

1 Bahá'u'lláh, The Kitab-i-Aqdas, p. 43, ¶ 64
2 'Abdu'l-Bahá, Selections from the Writings of 'Abdu'l-Bahá. P. 149
3 Spiritual abuse is perpetrated by ministers, priests, and those who practice judgmentalism and condemnation in the church.
4 My understanding is that human sexual feelings and attractions toward others, even within marriage, is normal, but to dwell on them would not be considered "keeping our thoughts pure," and to allow them to evolve into sexual fantasies or be acted upon would violate the principles of chastity. We cannot control our passing thoughts, but we can choose not to hold onto them. The sexual response is not to be repressed, but regulated.
"Of course many wayward thoughts come involuntarily to the mind and these are merely a result of weakness and are not blameworthy unless they become fixed or even worse, are expressed in improper acts." (Universal House of Justice 3/8/1981)
5 The Báb, Bahá'í Prayers, 2002, P. 227
6 Bahá'u'lláh, The Kitab-I-Aqdas, p. 25
7 Julie Swan, Personal Correspondence
8 Bahá'u'lláh, Gleanings from the Writings of Bahá'u'lláh, p. 236
9 The Báb, Bahá'í Prayers, 2002, p. 153
10 (Shoghi Effendi, The Advent of Divine Justice, p. 29)
11 Quran, Surah Al-Hadid (Iron) # 57: ayat 28&29.
12 I would like to give special thanks to Julie Swan, (school guidance counselor, retired, M.Ed. Counseling) for sharing her insights on these issues after reading an early draft of this book.
13 (Baha'u'llah, The Kitab-i-Iqan, p. 237)
14 'Abdu'l-Bahá, The Secret of Divine Civilization, p. 97
15 Bahá'u'lláh, Bahá'í Prayers, p. 16. (I looked up the word "hosts" in the dictionary and one of its meanings is an army (of idle fancies and vain imaginings.)
16 Bahá'u'lláh, Prayers and Meditations, p. 264
17 Thornton Chase – Before Abraham Was I Am, p. 11
18 Paul Lample, Creating a New Mind p. 31-32
19 Bahá'u'lláh, Bahá'í Prayers, 2002
20 Bahá'u'lláh, Proclamation of Bahá'u'lláh, p. 95
21 Bahá'u'lláh, Tablets of Bahá'u'lláh, p. 217, Book of the Covenant, Kitab-i-Ahd
22 'Abdu'l-Bahá, The Promulgation of Universal Peace, p. 262
23 Bahá'u'lláh, Bahá'í Prayers, Children's Section, p. 27
24 Tablets of Bahá'u'lláh, p. 111
25 Tablets of Bahá'u'lláh, p. 110-l11
26 'Abdu'l-Bahá, Selections from the Writings of 'Abdu'l-Bahá, p. 212
27 King James Bible, Psalms 19
28 King James Bible, Psalms 119

29 The King James Holy Bible, Ecclesiastes, 12:13
30 Bahá'u'lláh, Epistle to the Son of the Wolf, p. 42
31 'Abdu'l-Bahá, A Traveller's Narrative, p. 45
32 From a letter written on behalf of Shoghi Effendi to Alfred Lunt, 1936
33 'Abdu'l-Bahá, Promulgation of Universal Peace, p. 375
34 'Abdu'l-Bahá, Selections from the Writings of 'Abdu'l-Bahá, p. 237
35 'Abdu'l-Bahá, Bahá'i Prayers, 2002, p. 71
36 Bahá'u'lláh, Epistle to the Son of the Wolf, p. 42
37 'Abdu'l-Bahá, Promulgation of Universal Peace, p. 18
38 Bahá'u'lláh, Bahá'i Prayers, p. 68-69
39 Bahá'u'lláh, Synopsis and Codification of the Kitab-i-Aqdas, p. 24
40 Bahá'u'lláh, Gleanings from the Writings of Bahá'u'lláh, p. 204
41 'Abdu'l-Bahá, Tablets of the Divine Plan, p. 81
42 Selections from the Writings of 'Abdu'l-Bahá, p. 271
43 The community of the friends refers to the Bahá'i Community in which I live.
44 Bahá'u'lláh, Gleanings from the Writings of Bahá'u'lláh, p. 204
45 Bahá'u'lláh, The Kitab-i-Aqdas, p. 19
46 'Abdu'l-Bahá, Selections from the Writings of 'Abdu'l-Bahá, p. 70
47 Bahá'u'lláh, Bahá'i Prayers, 2002, p. 49
48 Bahá'u'lláh, Tablets of Bahá'u'lláh, p. 170
49 'Abdu'l-Bahá, the Promulgation of Universal Peace, p. 196
50 I have developed a social game called "The Boundary Sculpting Game" that is available through my website www.skylarkpubl.com
51 'Abdu'l-Bahá, Bahá'i Prayers, 2002, p. 217 Praise be unto Thee, O my God! These are Thy servants who are attracted by the fragrances of Thy mercifulness.
52 'Abdu'l-Bahá, SWAB, p. 132-133
53 Bahá'u'lláh, Gleanings from the Writings of Bahá'u'lláh, p. 93
54 'Abdu'l-Bahá, Promulgation of Universal Peace, p. 185
55 Bahá'u'lláh, Tablets of Bahá'u'lláh, p. 181
56 'Abdu'l-Bahá, Bahá'i Prayers, 2002, I cannot find the page!
57 Bahá'u'lláh, Gleanings from the Writings of Bahá'u'lláh, p. 340
58 'Abdu'l-Bahá, The Secret of Divine Civilization, p. 1
59 You can find a further exploration of this idea in my first book, **Assisting the Traumatized Soul**.
60 Bahá'u'lláh, Gleanings from the Writings of Bahá'u'lláh, p. 204
61 'Abdu'l-Bahá, The Secret of Divine Civilization, p. 19
62 'Abdu'l-Bahá, The Secret of Divine Civilization, p. 21
63 From a letter written on behalf of Shoghi Effendi to an individual believer, December 10, 1947, Compilation of Compilations.
64 Bahá'u'lláh, Gleanings from the Writings of Bahá'u'lláh, p. 296
65 'Abdu'l-Bahá, Selections from the Writings of Bahá'u'lláh, p. 141
66 'Abdu'l-Bahá, Bahá'i Prayers, 2002, p. 24
67 Bahá'u'lláh, Tablets of Bahá'u'lláh, p. 170
68 'Abdu'l-Bahá, A Traveller's Narrative, p. 63
69 Bahá'u'lláh, The Four Valleys, p. 58

70 Quoted by H.M.Balyuzi, Bahá'u'lláh, The King of Glory, p. 138
71 Bahá'u'lláh, Bahá'i Prayers, 2002, p. 159-160
72 Bahá'u'lláh, Gleanings from the Writings of Bahá'u'lláh, p. 323
73 'Abdu'l-Bahá, The Secret of Divine Civilization, p. 32 Included in this passage is a quotation from the Qur'án 39:12; 13:17.
74 Bahá'u'lláh, Kitab-i-Aqdas, p. 27, ¶ 17
75 Bahá'u'lláh, Tablets of Bahá'u'lláh, p. 200
76 Bahá'u'lláh, Bahá'i Prayers, 2002, p. 73-74
77 Bahá'u'lláh, Tablets of Bahá'u'lláh, p. 174
78 The Báb, Selections from the Writings of the Báb, p. 173
79 Tablets of 'Abdu'l-Bahá, v2, p. 278
80 Bahá'u'lláh, Prayers and Meditations, p. 27
81 'Abdu'l-Bahá, Secret of Divine Civilization, p. 33
82 'Abdu'l-Bahá, Some Answered Questions, p. 92
83 Bahá'u'lláh, Gleanings from the Writings of Bahá'u'lláh, p. 296
84 Bahá'u'lláh, Bahá'i Prayers, p. 74-75
85 Bahá'u'lláh, Gleanings from the Writings of Bahá'u'lláh, p. 326
86 The Báb, Selections from the Writings of the Báb, p. 190
87 Bahá'u'lláh, Gleanings from the Writings of Bahá'u'lláh, p. 204
88 Bahá'u'lláh, Epistle to the Son of the Wolf, p. 2
89 Bahá'u'lláh, Gleanings from the Writings of Bahá'u'lláh, p. 93
90 Bahá'u'lláh, Gleanings from the Writings of Bahá'u'lláh, p. 296
91 Bahá'u'lláh, Bahá'i Prayers, 2002, p. 75-76
92 Bahá'u'lláh, Kitab-i-Aqdas, p. 35, ¶ 45
93 'Abdu'l-Bahá, Abdu'l-Bahá in London, p. 48
94 Bahá'u'lláh, Prayers and Meditations, p. 75
95 Shoghi Effendi, Compilations, Lights of Guidance, p. 360, #1212
96 Bahá'u'lláh, Epistle to the Son of the Wolf, p. 26
97 Bahá'u'lláh, Gleanings from the Writings of Bahá'u'lláh, p. 5
98 Bahá'u'lláh, The Hidden Words of Bahá'u'lláh, #A9
99 Bahá'u'lláh, The Summons of the Lord of Hosts, p. 203, 5.51
100 Bahá'u'lláh, Bahá'i Prayers, 2002, 76
101 Bahá'u'lláh, Tablets of Bahá'u'lláh, Kitab-i-Ahd, p. 219
102 The Báb, Selections from the Writings of the Báb, p. 215
103 A newly translated extract from an unpublished Tablet revealed by 'Abdu'l-Bahá in the Persian language, cited in a letter dated November 26, 2003, from the Universal House of Justice to the members of the Bahá'í community in Iran).
104 Bahá'u'lláh, Prayers and Meditations, p. 111
105 Bahá'u'lláh, Epistle to the Son of the Wolf. P. 27
106 From a letter written on behalf of the Guardian to an individual believer, Octobr 19, 1947 Compilations, Lights of Guidance, p. 360
107 'Abdu'l-Bahá, Selections from the Writings of 'Abdu'l-Bahá, p. 4
108 Bahá'u'lláh, Gleanings from the Writings of Bahá'u'lláh, p. 262
109 'Abdu'l-Bahá, Selections from the Writings of 'Abdu'l-Bahá, p. 37
110 Bahá'u'lláh, Prayers and Meditations by Bahá'u'lláh, p. 231

Faithful

111 From a letter of the Universal House of Justice to two believers, May 22, 1996, Compilations, Lights of Guidance, p. 359
112 'Abdu'l-Bahá, Selections from the Writings of 'Abdu'l-Bahá, p. 73
113 'Abdu'l-Bahá, Selections from the Writings of 'Abdu'l-Bahá, p. 224
114 Bahá'u'lláh, The Hidden Words of Bahá'u'lláh, #A13
115 Bahá'u'lláh, Tablets of Bahá'u'lláh, p. 28
116 Baha'u'llah, Prayers and Meditations, p. 274
117 Letter written on behalf of Shoghi Effendi, Quoted in Universal House of Justice, letter dated 6 February 1973 to all National Spiritual Assemblies, Messages from the Universal House of Justice, 1963-1986, no. 126.2 and no. 126.7a
118 Bahá'u'lláh, Kitab-i-Aqdas, ¶ 4
119 Bahá'u'lláh, quoted in Shoghi Effendi, Advent of Divine Justice, p. 32 Note: in the Bahá'í Writings, the terms "handmaiden" and "servant" are used to describe stations of honor, not denigration.
120 'Abdu'l-Bahá, Selections from the Writings of 'Abdu'l-Bahá, nos. 86.1-86.2
121 'Abdu'l-Bahá, The Promulgation of Universal Peace, p. 176
122 Bahá'u'lláh, The Hidden Words of Bahá'u'lláh, #A22
123 Extract from a letter dated 22 May 1966 written on behalf of the Universal House of Justice to two individuals, in Lights of Guidance, no. 1219
124 All of the Prophets of the World religions were sent by one God: Krishna, Buddha, Zoroaster, Moses, Jesus, Muhammad, and Bahá'u'lláh.
125 SIA, Survivors of Incest Anonymous, http://www.siawso.org/Default.aspx?pageId=7166
126 Bahá'u'lláh, Prayers and Meditations by Bahá'u'lláh, p. 307
127 'Abdu'l-Baha, Compilations, Lights of Guidance, p. 225
128 'Abdu'l-Baha, Promulgation of Universal Peace, p. 235
129 'Abdu'l-Bahá, A Traveller's Narrative, p. 48
130 Bahá'u'lláh, Tablets of Bahá'u'lláh, p. 28
131 Bahá'u'lláh, Tablets of Bahá'u'lláh, p. 85
132 Bahá'u'lláh, Tablets of Bahá'u'lláh, p. 152
133 'Abdu'l-Bahá, The Promulgation of Universal Peace, p. 301
134 Bahá'u'lláh, Gleanings from the Writings of Bahá'u'lláh, p. 262
135 The Universal House of Justice, Messages, 1963 – 1986, p. 218
136 Bahá'u'lláh, Tablets of Bahá'u'lláh, p. 138
137 'Abdu'l-Bahá, A Traveller's Narrative, p. 46
138 Bahá'u'lláh, Epistle to the Son of the Wolf, p. 46
139 **Dua Kumayl** (Arabic: ÏÚÇÁ ßãíáý) (literally the Supplication of Kumayl) is a supplication famous among Shi'a for its perceived beauty and a traditional supplication in Shi'a Muslim spiritual practice.
140 Bahá'u'lllah, Gleanings From the Writings of Bahá'u'lláh, p. 178
141 'Abdu'l-Bahá, 'Abdu'l-Bahá in London, p. 19
142 Bahá'u'lláh, Tablets of Bahá'u'lláh, p. 169

143 Bahá'u'lláh, Gleanings from the Writings of Bahá'u'lláh, p. 104
144 Bahá'u'lláh, Kitab-i-Iqan, p. 210
145 From a letter dated 22 October 1949, written on behalf of the Guardian to an individual believer
146 The Báb, Bahá'i Prayers, 2002, p. 78-79
147 'Abdu'l-Bahá, The Secret of Divine Civilization, p. 104
148 'Abdu'l-Bahá, Foudations of World Unity, p. 16
149 Bahá'u'lláh, Tablets of Bahá'u'lláh, p. 157
150 Fire and Gold (A Compilation), p. 211
151 Bahá'u'lláh, Tablets of Bahá'u'lláh, p. 220
152 Shoghi Effendi, God Passes By, p. 214-215
153 Bahá'u'lláh, Gleanings from the Writings of Bahá'u'lláh, p. 129
154 Bahá'u'lláh, Tablets of Bahá'u'lláh, p. 95
155 'Abdu'l-Bahá, The Secret of Divine Civilization, p. 103
156 'Abdu'l-Bahá, Foundations of World Unity, p. 21
157 Bahá'u'lláh, Tablets of Bahá'u'lláh, p. 252
158 Bahá'u'lláh, Gleanings from the Writings of Bahá'u'lláh, p. 118
159 Bahá'u'lláh, Gleanings from the Writings of Bahá'u'lláh, p. 311
160 'Abdu'l-Bahá, Promulgation of Universal Peace, 336
161 'Abdu'l-Bahá, Foundations of World Unity, p. 16
162 Letter written on behalf of the Guardian to an individual believer, October 26, 1932, Bahá'i Youth: A Compilation, pp. 4 – 5, Lights of Guidance, p. 632
163 Bahá'u'lláh, The Hidden Words of Bahá'u'lláh, #A63
164 'Abdu'l-Bahá, The Promulgation of Universal Peace, p. 461
165 Bahá'u'lláh, Prayers and Meditations by Bahá'u'lláh, p. 22
165.5 Baha'u'llah, The Persian Hidden Words #29
166 'Abdu'l-Bahá, The Promulgation of Universal Peace, p. 294
167 'Abdu'l-Bahá, Foundations of World Unity, p. 110
168 'Abdu'l-Bahá, Prayer for Martyrs and their Families, Bahá'i Prayers, p. 294, 2002
169 Bahá'u'lláh, Fire Tablet, Bahá'i Prayers, p. 315
170 Baha'u'llah, Kitab-i-Aqdas, p. 84
171 'Abdu'l-Baha, Promulgation of Universal Peace, p. 453
172 Baha'u'llah, Prayers and Meditations, p. 235
173 'Abdu'l-Baha, Promulgation of Universal Peace, p. 239
174 Baha'u'llah, Gleanings from the Writings of Baha'u'llah
175 Bahá'u'lláh, The Hidden Words of Bahá'u'lláh, #P3
176 Bahá'u'lláh, Kitab-i-Aqdas, p. 97
177 'Abdu'l-Bahá, Some Answered Questions, p. 242
178 Bahá'u'lláh, Bahá'I Prayers, 2002, p. 96-97
179 'Abdu'l-Bahá, The Promulgation of Universal Peace, p. 178
180 Bahá'u'lllah, Gleanings from the Writings of Bahá'u'lláh, p. 291
181 Bahá'u'lláh, The Summons of the Lord of Hosts, p. 6
182 'Abdu'l-Bahá, Selections from the Writings of 'Abdu'l-Bahá, p. 123
183 Bahá'u'lláh, Prayers and Meditations by Bahá'u'lláh, p. 245

Faithful 133

184 Understanding Tests, Letter on behalf of the Universal House of Justice, July 17, 1989
185 On behalf of the Universal House of Justice: *The Compilation of Compilations, Vol. II,* "Preserving Bahá'i Marriages, p. 455
186 'Abdu'l-Bahá, The Promulgation of Universal Peace. P. 107
187 Baha'u'llah, Gleanings from the Writings of Baha'u'llah, p. 339
188 Bahá'u'lláh, The Summons of the Lord of Hosts, p. 8
189 'Abdu'l-Bahá, Memorials of the Faithful, p. 185. Shams-i-Duha means Lady of Light. She was a Babí and a Bahá'í teacher.
190 Bahá'u'lláh, Prayers and Meditations by Bahá'u'lláh, p. 266
191 'Abdu'l-Bahá, The Promulgation of Universal Peace, p. 69
192 Bahá'u'lláh, Gleanings from the Writings of Bahá'u'lláh, p. 340
193 Bahá'u'lláh, The Summons of the Lord of Hosts, p. 56
194 'Abdu'l-Bahá, A Traveller's Narrative, P. 48
195 Bahá'u'lláh, Prayers and Meditations by Bahá'u'lláh, p. 318
196 'Abdu'l-Bahá, Some Answered Questions, p. 236
197 Bahá'u'lláh, Prayers and Meditations by Bahá'u'lláh, p. 9
Note: Baha'is are required to "fast" from sunrise to sunset, for 19 days in the month of March.
198 Keith Clark, Capuchin, "Being Sexual... and Celebate, p. 108
199 'Abdu'l-Bahá, SWAB, p. 205
200 Bahá'u'lláh, Gleanings from the Writings of Bahá'u'lláh, p. 259
201 The Universal House of Justice, 1985 October, The Promise of World Peace, p. 5
202 'Abdu'l-Bahá, Bahá'i Prayers, 2002, p. 153

Acknowledgments

I am thankful for my patient husband who has taught me so much about honesty and justice, and encouraged me in my writing. The late Terry Cassiday, and my former editor, Ladan Cockshut, were instrumental in helping me learn that there is no shame in speaking the truth. I am in the debt of the National Spiritual Assembly of the United States and the Baha'i Publishing Trust for their support; in addition, friends Barb and John Grzelak, Kathleen and Kim Babb, and Mara Stafets, who believe in me and inspire me to continue in my writing when I lose my focus.

There are two people who guided me through the process of writing this book - social worker Julie Swan and therapist Mahin Pouryaghma. Their devotion to humanity and Baha'u'llah speaks volumes. They helped me bring out the vital treasures of reality.

I am grateful for the Revelation of Baha'u'llah, where I can satisfy my thirst for spirituality and find respite from fantasy. And a BIG thank you to Justice St. Rain at Special Ideas for giving me this wonderful opportunity to share experiences of my life once again.

Phyllis K. Peterson

skylarkpp@aol.com
www.skylarkpubl.com

www.ingramcontent.com/pod-product-compliance
Lightning Source LLC
LaVergne TN
LVHW051127080426
835510LV00018B/2284